MY COOKING CLASS
SEAFOOD BASICS

A FIREFLY BOOK

Published by Firefly Books Ltd. 2012

First printing

Publisher Cataloging-in-Publication Data (U.S.)

Fawcett, Abi.
Seafood basics : 86 recipes illustrated step by step / Abi Fawcett ; photography by Deirdre Rooney.
[256] p. : col. photos. ;   cm.
Includes index.
ISBN-13: 978-1-55407-941-4 (pbk.)
1. Cooking (Seafood).   I. Rooney, Deirdre. II. Title.
641.692 dc23   TX747.F394 2012

Library and Archives Canada Cataloguing in Publication

Fawcett, Abi
Seafood basics : 86 recipes illustrated step by step / Abi Fawcett
Includes index.
ISBN-13: 978-1-55407-941-4
1. Cooking (Seafood). 2. Cookbooks. I. Title.
TX747.F37 2012   641.6'92   C2012-901743-4

Published in the United States by
Firefly Books (U.S.) Inc.
P.O. Box 1338, Ellicott Station
Buffalo, New York 14205

Published in Canada by
Firefly Books Ltd.
66 Leek Crescent
Richmond Hill, Ontario L4B 1H1

Printed in China

MY COOKING CLASS
SEAFOOD BASICS

86 RECIPES
ILLUSTRATED STEP BY STEP

ABI FAWCETT

PHOTOGRAPHY BY DEIRDRE ROONEY

✳ ✳ ✳

FIREFLY BOOKS

INTRODUCTION

Wherever I've been on my travels I have enjoyed eating many seafood dishes and have noticed that the delicate taste of fish needs to be complemented perfectly so that a wonderful flavor can come through. The vast array of fish in many countries has meant that culinary flavors from across the globe can be used on the same type of fish with endless possibilities.

With their nutritional content, particularly their richness in Omega-3 oils, fish should be an integral part of our diet. However, buying and cooking fish seems a daunting prospect for many, and so fish and seafood seem to be rarely featured on the weekly household menu. But I feel that once you begin cooking fish and enjoying the benefits it brings, you will want to do it more and more.

Cooking fish can be very simple. Through the years I've come to realize the absolute importance of correct cooking methods. Timing is essential, as overcooked fish will undoubtedly ruin the dish, but the more you cook fish the better you will be at recognizing just exactly when your fish is ready to eat.

Don't lose hope, help is here and with this step-by-step book many of the pitfalls that can happen when cooking with fish can be overcome. By following the stages of each recipe, a wonderful dish that you can enjoy and be proud of accomplishing is just around the corner.

I hope you enjoy cooking fish and shellfish with me and also discovering a world of seafood delights. With these simple recipes, your next dinner party is sure to have a seafood theme!

CONTENTS

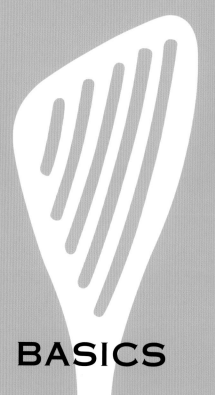

BASICS

TECHNIQUES

1 2
3 4

HOW TO STEAM

✤ BEST FISH TO USE : RED MULLET FILLETS , SEA BREAM FILLETS, SEA BASS FILLETS,
RED SNAPPER FILLETS, GRAY MULLET FILLETS, SOLE FILLETS ✤

1 Put 2 medium-sized fillets on a board, season well – this will increase the flavor.
2 Brush the fish with melted butter.
3 Put the fish into a steamer and steam over low heat for 3–4 minutes, or until cooked through.
4 Serve with a squeeze of lemon.

TIPS :

Some easy seasonings are crushed fennel seeds
and cayenne pepper.

Steaming is a great way to cook delicate fish
and a healthy option too.

1 2
3 4

HOW TO PAN-FRY

✦ BEST FISH TO USE : THICK PIECE POLLACK FILLET, SKIN ON, SCALED, ABOUT 8 OUNCES (250 G),
FARMED COD FILLET, SALMON FILLET, HADDOCK FILLET, HAKE FILLET ✦

1 Put the fish on a board, season and drizzle over a little oil.
2 Heat a non-stick frying pan over medium heat. Put the fish in the pan, skin side down and fry
   for about 2–3 minutes, or until the fillets are opaque at the edges.
3 Gently turn the fish over and fry for a further 1–2 minutes, or until firm to touch.
4 Serve the pan-fried fish with a squeeze of lemon.

TIP :
Your fish will fall apart if overcooked and
   the skin will burn if cooked on too high a
   temperature.

1 2
3 4

HOW TO GRILL

➤ BEST FISH TO USE : 4 SARDINES SCALED AND GUTTED, WITH HEADS ➤

IN ADVANCE : Preheat the grill to high.
1 Lay the fish skin side up on an oiled baking tray and season.
2 Drizzle olive oil over the fish and cook under the hot grill for 1–2 minutes until golden.
3 Turn the fish over and cook for a further 1–2 minutes until cooked through.
4 Serve the sardines with a squeeze of lemon.

TIP :
This is the easiest, most simple and delicious way of cooking fresh sardines.

1 2
3 4

HOW TO BAKE

➤ BEST FISH TO USE : SEA BASS, RED MULLET, MACKEREL, TROUT, PLAICE ➤

IN ADVANCE : Preheat the oven to 400°F (200°C).

1 Place 1 medium whole fish on a board and, using a sharp knife, make about 4 scores in the skin, then remove any fins with scissors.

2 Rub a little oil on the fish, season outside and inside the belly and put on a baking tray.

3 Bake the fish in the preheated oven for 20–25 minutes, or until the skin is crispy and the flesh feels firm to touch.

4 Serve the whole fish with lemon wedges and a drizzle of oil.

TIP :
If you overcook the fish it will become too dry.

1 2
3 4

HOW TO BARBECUE OR CHARGRILL

➥ BEST FISH TO USE : MACKEREL FILLETS, SEA BASS FILLETS, RED SNAPPER FILLETS,
TROUT FILLETS, JOHN DORY FILLETS, GRAY MULLET FILLETS ◁

IN ADVANCE : Heat the barbecue or chargrill pan.

1 Season medium-sized fish fillets and drizzle over a little oil.

2 Place the fish skin side down on the barbecue or chargrill pan and cook for 1–2 minutes.

3 Turn the fish over and cook for a further 1–2 minutes, or until the flesh is firm to touch and the skin remains crispy.

4 Serve the fillets with a drizzle of extra virgin olive oil and lemon wedges.

TIP :
The fish will fall apart if overcooked.

1 2
3 4

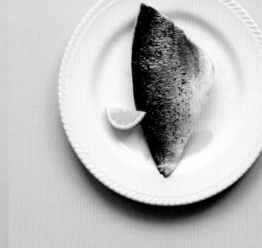

HOW TO COOK EN PAPILLOTE

➤ BEST FISH TO USE : RED MULLET FILLETS, SEA BREAM FILLETS, SEA BASS FILLETS,
RED SNAPPER FILLETS, GRAY MULLET FILLETS, HAKE FILLET ◄

IN ADVANCE : Preheat the oven to 400°F (200°C) Cut out 1 piece of greaseproof paper and 1 piece of foil, each about roughly 12 inches (30 cm) in diameter.

1 Put medium-sized fillets of fish on top of the greaseproof paper with the foil underneath.

2 Season, then drizzle with oil and add any flavors here (see tip, right).

3 Fold the greaseproof in half with the foil, then fold over the top part, enclosing it completely. Put on a baking tray and bake in the oven for 5–10 minutes.

4 Remove from the oven and carefully lift onto a serving plate. Serve with lemon and a drizzle of olive oil.

TIP :
Add flavors such as slices of red chili, lemongrass or lemon slices.

RAW & CURED

1

SALMON GRAVLAX

✦ SERVES 8–10 (AS A STARTER) • PREPARATION : 10–20 MINUTES • CHILLING : 2–3 DAYS ✦

½ cup (100 g) coarse salt
⅓ cup (75g) caster sugar
1 bunch of dill, roughly chopped
Peel of 1 lemon
Peel of 1 orange

1 tablespoon (15 ml) fennel seeds
1 tablespoon (15 ml) crushed mixed
  peppercorns
1½ pounds (750 g) salmon fillets, with skin
  on and pin boned

2 tablespoons (30 ml) gin

| 1 | Mix together the salt, sugar, dill, citrus peels, fennel and peppercorns. | 2 | Spread the mixture over the salmon to cover completely, then pour on the gin. | 3 | Tightly wrap the fish in cling wrap, put a weight on top and chill for 2–3 days. |
| 4 | Brush some of the curing mixture off the fish and pat dry. | 5 | Starting at tail, cut under fillet separating the skin and cut along fillet (see tip). | 6 | Turn the fish over and trim off any brown bits. ➤ |

7	Using a long, sharp knife, carefully carve thin diagonal slivers off the salmon.	**TIP** ✳ To remove the skin in step 5, using a sharp knife and starting at the tail end, carefully cut under the fillet to separate the skin, then, holding onto the skin, continue to cut along the length of the fillet.

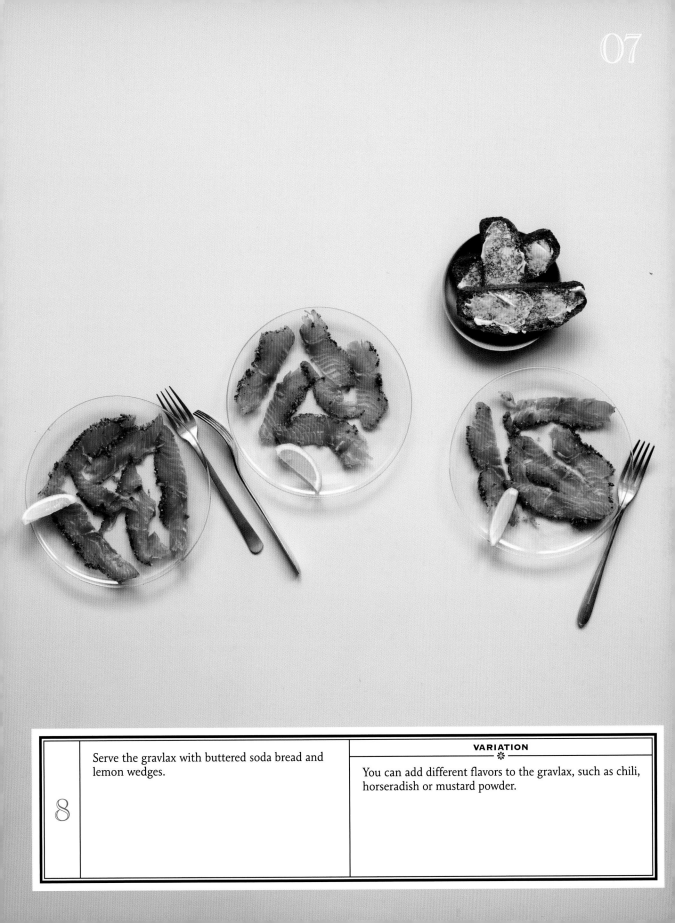

			VARIATION
8	Serve the gravlax with buttered soda bread and lemon wedges.		You can add different flavors to the gravlax, such as chili, horseradish or mustard powder.

TUNA CARPACCIO

❧ SERVES 4 (AS A STARTER) • PREPARATION : 10 MINUTES • COOKING : N/A ❧

10 ounces (300 g) middle-cut tuna loin
Pinch of black pepper
Pinch of sea salt flakes
Drizzle of extra virgin olive oil
1 cup (40 g) arugula

IN ADVANCE :
Chill 4 serving plates

1 2
3 4

1	Thinly slice the tuna with a very sharp knife – you may need to use a mallet to bash the tuna a little – and place onto the platter.	2	Season with the pepper and salt and drizzle with the oil.
3	Scatter the arugula leaves on top.	4	Serve with lemon wedges and sliced avocado.

SEARED TUNA & POPPY SEED

❧ SERVES 2–4 • PREPARATION : 10 MINUTES + 30 MINUTES CHILLING • COOKING : 5–6 MINUTES ❧

2 x 4 ounce (120 g) tuna, cut lengthways
2 tablespoons (30 ml) poppy seeds
1 tablespoon (15 ml) sesame seeds
Salt and black pepper
1 tablespoon (15 ml) vegetable oil

DRESSING :
1 tablespoon (15 ml) soy sauce
1 tablespoon (15 ml) grated ginger
1 tablespoon (15 ml) honey
2 tablespoons (30 ml) mirin
3 tablespoons (45 ml) vegetable oil

IN ADVANCE :
Preheat a medium-sized frying pan.

1	Roll the tuna in the poppy and sesame seeds and seasoning.	2	Add the oil to the hot pan and sear the tuna for 8–10 seconds on each side.	3	Cool slightly, then roll the tuna tightly in cling wrap and chill for 30 minutes.
4	Mix all the dressing ingredients together.	5	Unwrap the tuna and thinly slice it, then arrange on serving plates.	6	Serve the tuna with the dressing accompanied with cucumber and radish.

SEA BASS CEVICHE

❧ SERVES 4 (AS A STARTER) • PREPARATION : 5 MINUTES • MARINATING : 2–3 MINUTES ❧

1 head of fennel
1 pomegranate, seeds removed
½ bunch of mint, leaves only
Juice of 1 lime
Juice of 1 orange

1 teaspoon sugar
3 tablespoons (45 ml) extra virgin olive oil
Good pinch of salt and black pepper
12 ounce (350 g) sea bass fillets, pin boned

1 2
3 4

1	Using a mandoline, thinly slice the fennel. Put in a bowl with the pomegranate seeds and mint and mix together.	2	In a separate bowl, combine the citrus juices and sugar together with the oil, and season with salt and pepper.
3	Thinly slice the sea bass and place on a large serving platter.	4	Pour on the dressing and leave to marinate for 2–3 minutes. Serve with the fennel and pomegranate salad.

PICKLED SARDINES ESCABECHE

❖ SERVES 4 • PREPARATION : 10 MINUTES + 6 HOURS MARINATING • COOKING : 5 MINUTES + 20 MINUTES COOLING ❖

2 tablespoons (30 ml) olive oil
Salt and black pepper
7 whole sardines, with heads removed, gutted
   and scaled

1 teaspoon coriander seeds
1 teaspoon mustard seeds
Good pinch of chili flakes
3 bay leaves

4 shallots, thinly sliced
1 garlic clove, thinly sliced
½ cup (125 ml) white wine
½ cup (125 ml) cider vinegar

1	Heat a little oil. Season fish, put skin side down and fry for 2 minutes on each side.	2	Transfer the sardines to a deep dish.
4	Add the shallots and garlic and cook for 2 minutes. Add the wine and vinegar.	5	Pour the marinade over the fish. Cool completely then chill for 6 hours.

3	Heat a little more oil, add the spices and bay leaves and cook until fragrant.
6	Serve the fish with flatbread and some of the pickle marinade.

HOT SMOKED SALMON

❖ SERVES 2 • PREPARATION : 5–10 MINUTES • COOKING : 8–10 MINUTES ❖

1 cup (100 g) white rice
½ cup (100 g) loose tea
⅓ cup (75 g) soft brown sugar
Salt and black pepper
2 x 8 ounce (250 g) salmon fillets, skin on
1 tablespoon (15 ml) liquid honey

IN ADVANCE :
Line the base of a large wok (with a lid) with
   foil. You will also need a wire rack.

1	Put the rice, tea and sugar into the foil-lined wok and mix together well.	2	Put a wire rack over the wok. Cover with the lid and put over medium heat.	3	Season the fish on both sides and brush with a little honey.
4	Lay the fish skin side up onto the wire rack and place the lid on top.	5	Cook for 4–5 minutes. Take off the heat and allow to cool for 5 minutes.	6	Serve the fish with avocado, lemon and a drizzle of extra virgin olive oil.

13

HOMEMADE PICKLED HERRINGS

➤ SERVES 4 • PREPARATION : 10 MINUTES + 2–3 HOURS MARINATING • COOKING : 5 MINUTES + 3 DAYS PICKLING

⅓ cup (60 g) sea salt
6 large, fresh herrings, scaled, gutted and
  filleted (making sure no bones are left in
  the fish)

MARINADE :
2 cups (500 ml) white wine vinegar
1 teaspoon mustard seeds
1 cup (250 ml) white wine
Peel of 1 orange

2 tablespoons (30 ml) brown sugar
1 tablespoon (15 ml) mixed peppercorns
6–8 bay leaves

1 2
3 4

1	Dissolve the salt in 2 cups (500 ml) cold water to make brine, then add the fillets. Leave for 2–3 hours.	2	Put all the marinade ingredients in a saucepan and slowly bring to a boil. Reduce the heat and simmer for 1 minute. Cool completely.
3	Drain the herring fillets from the brine, put onto paper towels to dry them. Roll them up, skin side out and secure with a cocktail stick.	4	Put the herring rolls into sterilized large preserving jars. ➤

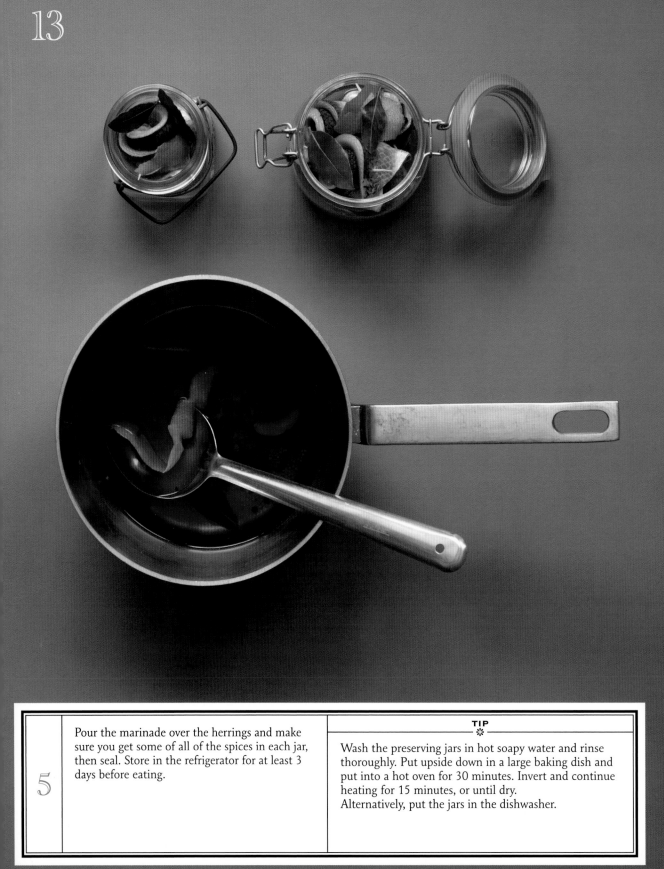

5	Pour the marinade over the herrings and make sure you get some of all of the spices in each jar, then seal. Store in the refrigerator for at least 3 days before eating.

TIP

Wash the preserving jars in hot soapy water and rinse thoroughly. Put upside down in a large baking dish and put into a hot oven for 30 minutes. Invert and continue heating for 15 minutes, or until dry.
Alternatively, put the jars in the dishwasher.

	To serve, drain the fillets from their marinade and accompany with slices of fresh crusty bread and parsley leaves.	**NOTE** ❋
6		Ideally, it is best to leave the herrings pickling in the marinade for about 5–10 days before eating and then they can last up to 2 weeks in sterilized jars.

SOUPS & STEWS

2

TRADITIONAL

WORLD

BOUILLABAISSE

❖ SERVES 6–8 • PREPARATION : 10 MINUTES • COOKING : 20–25 MINUTES ❖

1 pound (500 g) mixed fish, skin on and pin boned
2 tablespoons (30 ml) extra virgin olive oil
2 onions, thinly sliced
1 leek and 1 celery stick, thinly sliced
1 fennel bulb, thinly sliced
4 garlic cloves, finely sliced

14 ounce (400 g) can plum tomatoes
Pinch of saffron and peel of 1 orange
2 bay leaves and 1 teaspoon thyme leaves
3½ cups (800 ml) fish stock
Salt and black pepper
7 ounces (200 g) mussels, cleaned and debearded

10 ounces (300 g) mix of langoustines and jumbo shrimp

ROUILLÉ :
2 roasted red peppers
⅔ cup (150 g) mayonnaise
1 garlic clove

1 2
3 4

1	Cut the fish into large pieces.	2	Heat the oil in a heavy-based casserole, add the onions, leeks, celery, fennel and garlic and cook gently for 5 minutes until soft.	
3	Add the tomatoes, saffron, orange peel, bay leaves, thyme, stock and seasoning. Bring to a boil, reduce the heat and simmer for 15 minutes.	4	Meanwhile, blend the ingredients for the rouillé for 1 minute in a food processor. Season to taste and set aside.	➤

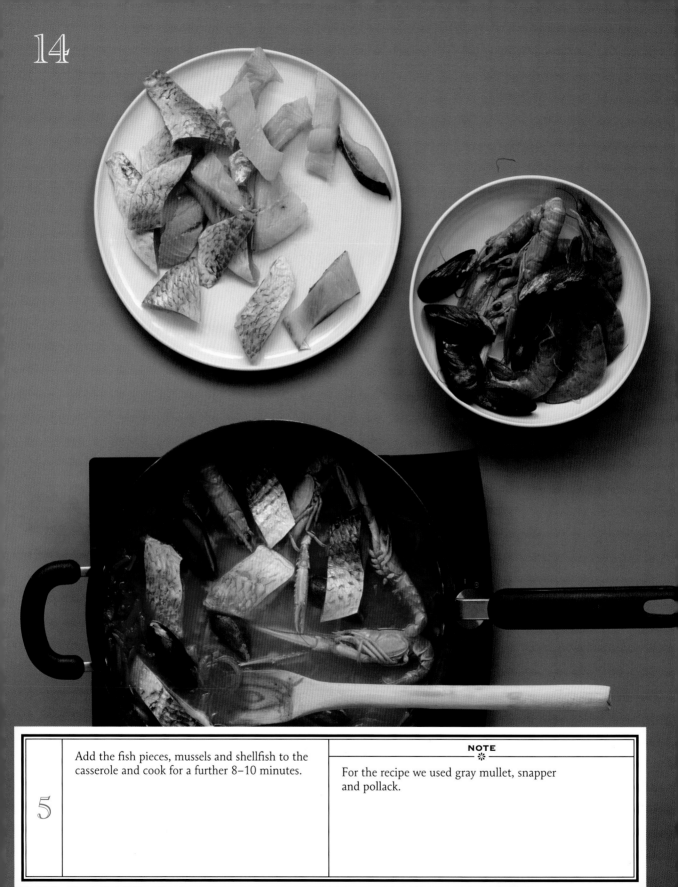

5 Add the fish pieces, mussels and shellfish to the casserole and cook for a further 8–10 minutes.

NOTE
✳

For the recipe we used gray mullet, snapper and pollack.

		TIP ✻
6	Sprinkle on some chopped parsley and serve with croûtons and the rouillé.	Cut the fish to the same size so it will cook at the same time and be sure to use a large pan so the fish is not overcrowded while cooking.

CLASSIC FISH STEW

➤ SERVES 4–6 • PREPARATION : 10 MINUTES • COOKING : 10 MINUTES ➤

2 tablespoons (30 ml) olive oil
2 garlic cloves, sliced
1 red chili, sliced
8 ounces (250 g) snapper, cut into large pieces
7 ounces (200 g) salmon, cut into large pieces,
 skin on and pin boned

7 tablespoons (100 ml) white wine
5 ounces (150 g) clams, cleaned
7 ounces (200 g) mussels, cleaned and
 debearded
6 large shrimp, raw
14 ounce (400 g) can chopped tomatoes

1 small bunch of basil
2 cups (100 g) baby spinach
Salt and black pepper

1	Heat the oil in a pan, add the garlic and chili and fry gently for 1 minute.	2	Add the fish and white wine and cook for 1 minute until the wine reduces.	3	Add the shellfish (clams, mussels and large shrimp), tomatoes and basil.
4	Cover with a lid and cook for 5–6 minutes.	5	Uncover, add the spinach to the pan and cook for a further 1 minute.	6	Season to taste and serve in large soup plates with crusty bread.

CRAB BISQUE

⇻ SERVES 4–6 • PREPARATION : 10 MINUTES • COOKING : 50 MINUTES ⇺

2 pounds (1 kg) crab
¼ cup (50 g) butter
⅓ cup (50 g) onion, chopped
⅓ cup (50 g) celery, chopped
3 bay leaves
2 tablespoons (30 ml) Cognac

14 ounce (400 g) can plum tomatoes
1 teaspoon tomato purée
5 tablespoons (75 ml) dry white wine
7½ cups (1.75 L) fish stock
5 tablespoons (75 ml) thick double cream
Pinch of cayenne pepper

Juice of ¼ lemon
Salt and black pepper

1	Put the crab into a pot of boiling water and cook for 8–10 minutes. Drain and allow to cool slightly.	2	Chop the crab roughly using a large knife and removing any gills, (see cooking & preparing a crab, 57).
3	Melt the butter in a heavy-based pot, add the chopped onion, celery and the bay leaves and cook gently for 5 minutes.	4	Add the crab and Cognac to the pan and cook for a few minutes. ➢

5	Add the tomatoes, tomato purée, wine, and stock. Bring to a boil, then reduce the heat and simmer for 30 minutes.	6	Working in 2–3 batches, blend the mixture in a liquidizer or food processor. Don't worry if there is any shell as it will be strained.
7	Strain the soup through a conical strainer pushing as much liquid through as you can with the back of a ladle to extract all the juices.	8	Return the bisque to a pot and add the cream, then season to taste with cayenne pepper, lemon juice, salt and black pepper.

9   Serve the bisque in bowls.

NOTE

❈

Accompany the bisque with slices of crusty bread.

FISH & SEAFOOD RAGU

❧ SERVES 4–6 • PREPARATION : 10 MINUTES • COOKING : 40–45 MINUTES + 10 MINUTES COOLING ❧

2 pounds (1 kg) mussels, scrubbed and debearded
1 cup (200 ml) white wine
A little olive oil
1 onion, sliced

2 garlic cloves, sliced
2 celery sticks, sliced
2 x 14 ounce (400 g) cans plum tomatoes
1 bunch of basil
2 tablespoons (30 ml) capers

14 ounces (400 g) tuna
14 ounces (400 g) pappardelle pasta, cooked according to the package instructions

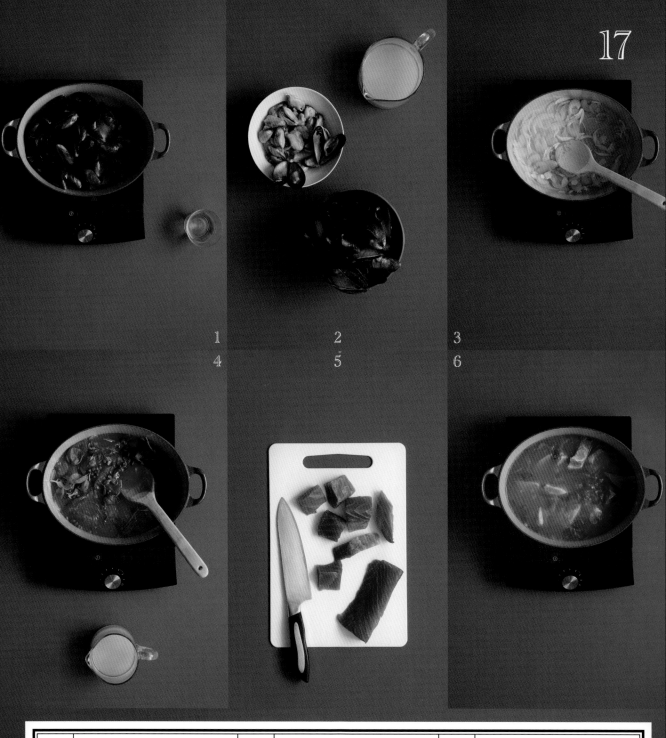

1
4

2
5

3
6

1	Put the mussels and wine in a large heavy-based pot and cook for 4–5 minutes.	2	Allow the mussels to cool, then remove them from the shells. Keep the juices.	3	Heat a little oil in the pot and cook the onion, garlic and celery for 5–10 minutes.	
4	Add the tomatoes, basil, mussel juice and capers and cook for 10–15 minutes.	5	Roughly chop the tuna into large pieces.	6	Add the tuna to the pot and cook for 20–25 minutes.	➤

7	Add the shelled mussels to the pot and the cooked pasta and cook gently for about 1–2 minutes until the mussels and pasta are warmed through.	**TIP** ✱ To prepare mussels, rinse them under cold running water, then scrub them with a stiff brush to get rid of grit and barnacles. Pull away the hairy beard and if any mussels are open tap them with a knife. If they don't close, throw them away. After cooking the mussels in step 1, discard any that have not opened.

| 8 | Sprinkle with basil leaves and a drizzle of extra virgin olive oil and serve. | **VARIATION** ❋
 Try using linguine or tagliatelle instead of pappardelle. |

MOROCCAN FISH TAGINE

❧ SERVES 4 • PREPARATION : 10–15 MINUTES • COOKING : 20–25 MINUTES ❧

2 tablespoons (30 ml) vegetable oil
2 onions, finely chopped
2 garlic cloves, finely sliced
1 teaspoon cumin seeds
1 teaspoon ground ginger
1 cinnamon stick

1 preserved lemon, roughly chopped
⅓ cup (75 g) pitted green olives
1 tablespoon (15 ml) harissa chili paste
1¼ cups (300 ml) fish stock
Pinch of saffron strands
1 pound (500 g) mixed firm monkfish and

gurnard, skin removed and pin boned
14 ounce (400 g) can chopped tomatoes

IN ADVANCE :
Preheat the oven to 325°F (170°C).

18

| 1 | Heat the oil in a pan and cook the onions and garlic gently until soft and golden. | 2 | Add the cumin, ginger, cinnamon, lemon and olives and cook for 2 minutes. | 3 | Add the harissa and cook for 1 minute. |
| 4 | Stir in the stock and saffron and bring to a gentle simmer. Transfer to a tagine. | 5 | Add the fish and tomatoes, cover and bake in the oven for 15–20 minutes. | 6 | Sprinkle coriander sprigs over the tagine and serve with steamed couscous. |

LOUISIANA SEAFOOD GUMBO

❧ SERVES 4–6 • PREPARATION : 10–15 MINUTES • COOKING : 30–35 MINUTES ❧

2 tablespoons (30 g) butter
2 tablespoons (30 ml) vegetable oil
¼ cup (30 g) plain flour
1 onion, chopped
1 celery stick, chopped
1 green pepper, chopped

7 ounces (200 g) chorizo sausage, thickly sliced
1 tablespoon (15 ml) Cajun spice
1 bay leaf
4 large tomatoes, roughly chopped
4 cups (1 L) chicken stock

14 ounces (400 g) jumbo shrimp, raw, peeled
10 ounces (300 g) live clams
Salt and black pepper

1 2
3 4

1	In a large heavy-based pot, melt the butter, oil and flour and cook for 2–3 minutes, or until dark brown.	2	Add the onion, celery, green pepper and chorizo and cook for 3–4 minutes.	
3	Add the Cajun spice and bay leaf and cook for a further 1 minute.	4	Reduce the heat, add the tomatoes and stock and cook for 15–20 minutes, stirring occasionally.	➤

| 5 | Add the jumbo shrimp and clams to the pot and cook for 4–5 minutes, or until cooked. | **TIP**
✻
To prepare clams, scrub them under cold running water with a stiff brush. After cooking the clams in step 7, discard any clams that are not open. |

| 6 | Season to taste with salt and pepper, then serve in large soup plates garnished with parsley and accompanied with rice. | **NOTE**
❋
Cajun spice can be used as a rub on meat and fish or added to dishes as a flavoring. It is readily available in supermarkets. |

WHOLE FISH

3

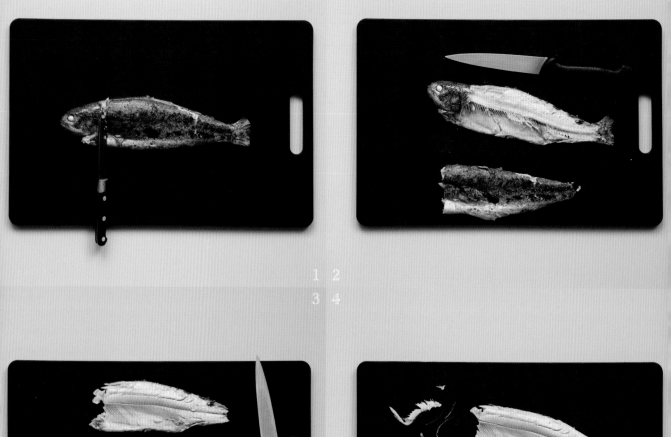

1 2
3 4

FILLETING A COOKED ROUND FISH

1	Run a knife down the length of the fish between the 2 fillets along back bone and back of head.	2	Gently ease the fillets apart away from the bones.
3	Lift the fillets in from one side and repeat with the other side.	4	Remove any small bones with tweezers and serve.

1 2
3 4

FILLETING A COOKED FLAT FISH

1	Work down either side, trap lateral bones that run down outside edge and drag them away.	2	Run knife down center and ease fillets away from bones; leave attached to outside of fish.
3	Take hold of the bones at the head end, and the fillets will fall back into place.	4	Cut the fillets in half (you should have 4 fillets) and serve with or without the roe.

ROASTED RED MULLET

➤ SERVES 4 • PREPARATION : 10 MINUTES • COOKING : 20–30 MINUTES + 15 MINUTES COOLING ➤

4 whole red mullet, gutted and scaled
3 red onions, sliced into wedges
2 fennel bulbs, thickly sliced
2 zucchinis, thickly sliced
2 tablespoons (30 ml)olive oil
Salt and black pepper

PASTE :
10 on-the-vine cherry tomatoes
2 whole red chilies, seeded (optional)
4 garlic cloves, peeled
2 tablespoons (30 ml) olive oil
½ teaspoon fennel seeds

IN ADVANCE :
Preheat the oven to 400°F (200°C).

1 2
3 4

1	For the paste, put the tomatoes, chilies, garlic and 1 tablespoon oil on aluminum foil and roast for 10 minutes. Allow to cool completely.	2	Transfer the roasted tomato mix to a pestle and mortar, add the fennel seeds and seasoning and mash together to make a paste.
3	Put the red mullet on a board and score each side of the fish 3 times with a sharp knife, then trim off any fish fins with scissors.	4	Add the rest of the oil to the paste and mix together, then spoon over the fish. ➤

| 5 | Place the vegetables in a roasting tray and drizzle with the oil. Season, then place the fish on top and roast in the oven for 15–20 minutes. | **TIP**
❋

To scale a fish, hold the fish by the tail and, using the back of a knife, scrape off the scales from the tail to the head. To gut a fish, slit the belly open from the gills to the tail, then, using your fingers, loosen the innards from the belly and behind the gills and pull them out and throw them away. |

1   2   3

4   5   6

1	Using a sharp knife and firmly holding the fish score it 3–4 times on one side.	2	Stuff each fish cavity with some of the dill and the lemon slices.	3	Lay the remaining dill on top, sprinkle with fennel and top with a lemon slice.
4	Wrap 4 slices of pancetta around the fish and brush with oil. Season.	5	Bake for 10–12 minutes until the pancetta is golden and the fish is cooked.	6	Serve with steamed greens and lemon.

PLAICE WITH TOMATO & THYME

❧ SERVES 2–4 • PREPARATION : 10 MINUTES • COOKING : 20–25 MINUTES ❧

1 whole plaice, about 1½ pounds (700 g), trimmed, skinned and roe removed
Salt and black pepper
1 tablespoon (15 ml) olive oil
14 ounces (400 g) baby plum tomatoes
1 small bunch of thyme

3 garlic cloves thinly sliced

DRESSING :
Juice of one orange
1 teaspoon red wine vinegar
3 tablespoons (45 ml) extra virgin olive oil

IN ADVANCE :
Preheat the oven to 400°F (200°C).

6

Serve the fish with the vegetables on the side and spoon over any of the remaining sauce.

VARIATION
❀

Use any combination of summer vegetables such as red pepper instead of the fennel, if you like.

TROUT BAKED WITH LEMON

❧ SERVES 2 • PREPARATION : 10 MINUTES • COOKING : 10–12 MINUTES ❧

2 x 8 ounce (250 g) rainbow trout, gutted and
  cleaned
1 small bunch of dill
1 lemon, cut into slices
1 tablespoon (15 ml) crushed fennel seeds

8 slices pancetta
4 tablespoons (60 ml) olive oil
Salt and black pepper

IN ADVANCE
Preheat the oven to 425°F (220°C).

1 2
3 4

1	Score the fish with a sharp knife and season with salt and pepper.	2	Put the fish on a tray and drizzle with the oil. Add the tomatoes, thyme and garlic and cook in the oven for 20–25 minutes.
3	Mix all the ingredients for the dressing together in a small bowl and spoon over the cooked fish.	4	Remove the fillets from the fish (see filleting a cooked flat fish, 21). Serve with the tomatoes and juices.

STUFFED TURBOT WITH SHRIMP

➝ SERVES 4 • PREPARATION : 10–15 MINUTES • COOKING : 15–20 MINUTES ↢

2 pounds (1 kg) turbot, scaled and gutted
¼ cup (50 g) butter, melted
5 ounces (150 g) brown shrimp
2 garlic cloves, finely sliced

3 shallots, finely sliced
1 small bunch of flat leaf parsley, chopped
Salt and black pepper
Olive oil, for drizzling

IN ADVANCE :
Preheat the oven to 400°F (200°C).

1 2
3 4

1	Put the fish on a chopping board and, using the tip of the knife, gently run it down the middle of the fish.	2	Now part the fish fillet from the bone with the tip of the knife, about 1½–2 inches (4–5 cm) deep on both sides to make a pocket.	
3	Put the melted butter, shrimps, garlic and shallots into a bowl and mix well. Add the parsley and season.	4	Transfer the fish to a large roasting pan and stuff the shrimp mixture into the pocket. Season the fish.	➤

| 5 | Drizzle on some oil and bake in the oven for 15–20 minutes, or until the fish is cooked. | **TIP**

The turbot should lay flat in the roasting pan so make sure it is big enough before using. |

| 6 | Remove the fillets from the fish (see filleting a cooked flat fish, 21), then serve with some of the shrimp stuffing and a lemon wedge. | **NOTE**
❋
You can serve this dish with a crisp green or mixed salad, if you like. |

ROASTED WHOLE SEA BASS

❖ SERVES 2–4 • PREPARATION : 10 MINUTES • COOKING : 20–25 MINUTES ❖

2 whole sea bass, about 8 ounces (250 g) each, cleaned
3 tablespoons (50 ml) olive oil
Salt and black pepper
2 yellow peppers, cut into large pieces

1 red pepper, cut into large pieces
1 pound (500 g) cherry tomatoes
¼ cup (50 g) anchovies, sliced

IN ADVANCE :
Preheat the oven to 400°F (200°C).

1 2
3 4

1	Slash the fish diagonally 4–5 times across the skin one way and then the other with a sharp knife. Trim off the fins.	2	Rub the fish generously with oil, then season well with salt and pepper.
3	Arrange the peppers, tomatoes and anchovies on a large baking tray. Put the fish on top and drizzle with the remaining oil.	4	Bake the fish in the oven for 20–25 minutes. Take the fish out of the oven, remove the head and serve with the vegetables and anchovies.

PLAICE WITH PEPPERCORNS

❖ SERVES 2–4 • PREPARATION : 5–10 MINUTES • COOKING : 20–30 MINUTES ❖

2 pounds (1 kg) plaice, scaled and gutted, skin on
3 white onions, finely sliced
½ cup (100 ml) fish stock
2 tablespoons (30 g) green peppercorns

Salt and black pepper
6 bay leaves
2 tablespoons (30 g) butter, cut into small pieces
2 tablespoons (30 ml) olive oil

IN ADVANCE :
Preheat the oven to 400°F (200°C).

1	Put the fish on a board with the skin side facing up and slash it with a sharp knife.	2	Put onions, stock and peppercorns in a large tray. Season the fish well and place on top. Add bay leaves, dot with butter and drizzle with oil.
3	Bake in the oven for 20–30 minutes, or until the fish is cooked.	4	Carefully lift the fish away from the bones (see filleting a cooked flat fish, 21), then serve with the juices poured over the fish.

SALT-ENCRUSTED SEA BASS

✦ SERVES 4 • PREPARATION : 5–10 MINUTES • COOKING : 20 MINUTES ✦

2–3 dried red chilies
Peel of 1 lemon
6 pounds (3 kg) sea salt
1 lemon, cut into slices
1 small bunch of parsley

2 sea bass, 12 ounces (350 g) each, scaled and
  gutted
2 egg whites

IN ADVANCE :
Preheat the oven to 400°F (200°C).

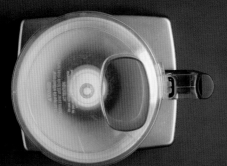

1 2
3 4

1	Blend the chilies, lemon peel and salt together in a food processor.	2	Put the lemon slices and parsley into the belly of the fish.	
3	Mix the flavored salt and egg whites together in a bowl.	4	Put half the salt mix into a shallow baking dish and put the fish on top. Cover the fish with the rest of the salt mix.	➤

		TIP
5	Bake in the oven for 20 minutes. Remove the fish from the oven and allow it to cool slightly. Break the salt crust with a knife and discard it. Scrape off the skin.	Make sure the fish is completely covered in the salt mixture in step 4.

6

Lift off the fillets from the fish and serve with green beans, lemon slices and a drizzle of oil.

TIP
❋

To carefully remove the fillets from the cooked fish see filleting a cooked round fish, 20.

BARBECUED MACKEREL

SERVES 2–4 • PREPARATION : 5–10 MINUTES • COOKING : 8–10 MINUTES

2 x 12 ounce (350 g) whole mackerel, scaled and gutted
Salt and black pepper
1 tablespoon (15 ml) olive oil
1 lime, cut into slices

2 garlic cloves, sliced
2 tablespoons (30 ml) honey
1 tablespoon (15 ml) soy sauce

IN ADVANCE :
Preheat a barbecue or a heavy-based grill pan to medium-high heat.

1 2
3 4

1	To prepare the fish, season and oil them slightly, then slash the skin diagonally 3 times with a sharp knife.	2	Put the lime slices and garlic into the belly of the fish.	
3	Lay the fish on top of the grill pan or barbecue and cook for 4–5 minutes pressing down on the fish with a fish slice.	4	Mix the honey and soy sauce together in a small bowl.	➤

5	Turn the fish over and brush with the honey mixture. Cook for a further 3–4 minutes.	**TIP** ❋ Make sure the grill pan is hot before cooking the fish. Press the fish down onto the grill pan with a fish slice or spatula to make sure it catches a little.

6. Put the fish on a serving dish and brush over any remaining honey mixture. Serve with coriander sprigs, lime wedges and sliced chili.

VARIATION
❋

Use lemon instead of lime, if you like.

GRILLED PLAICE WITH HARISSA

✦ SERVES 2 • PREPARATION : 5–10 MINUTES • COOKING : 6–8 MINUTES ✦

2 whole plaice, cleaned and gutted
¼ cup (50 g) butter, softened
1 tablespoon (15 ml) harissa chili paste
Salt and black pepper

IN ADVANCE :
Preheat the grill to high.

1	Remove the frills from the fish with scissors.	2	Score the fish on both sides and along the middle like the veins of a leaf.	3	Mix the butter and harissa together in a small bowl.
4	Place the fish onto a baking tray and dot the butter over the top, then season.	5	Place under the hot grill and cook for 6–8 minutes, or until golden brown.	6	Serve with lemon and salad and spoon on some juices from the cooked fish.

SOLE À LA MEUNIÈRE

❧ SERVES 2 • PREPARATION : 10 MINUTES • COOKING : 12 MINUTES ❧

½ cup (100 g) butter
½ cup (70 g) plain flour
Salt and black pepper

1 whole sole, about 14 ounces (400 g),
  gutted with dark skin removed (ask your
  fishmonger)
2 tablespoons (30 ml) lemon juice
1 tablespoon (15 ml) chopped parsley

IN ADVANCE :
Preheat a large frying pan over medium heat.

1 2
3 4

1	To clarify the butter, put the butter into a pan and heat gently to let the impurities come to the surface, skimming these off with a spoon.	2	Put the flour on a tray and season. Add the fish and coat until the fish is lightly dusted with the seasoned flour.
3	Heat half of the clarified butter in the frying pan and fry the fish skin side down for 4 minutes.	4	Turn the fish over and cook for a further 4 minutes, or until golden. ➤

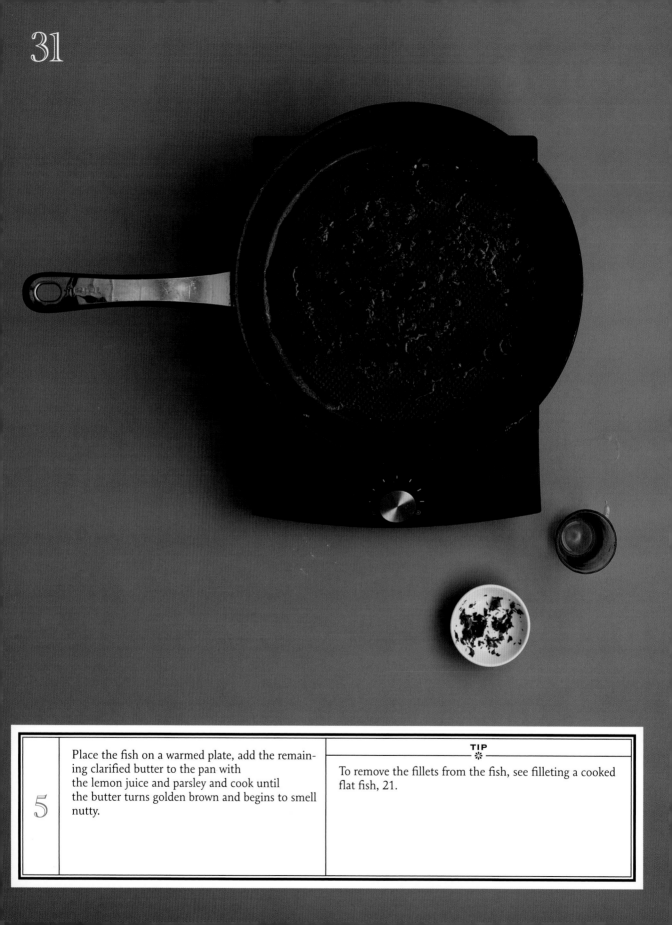

| 5 | Place the fish on a warmed plate, add the remaining clarified butter to the pan with the lemon juice and parsley and cook until the butter turns golden brown and begins to smell nutty. | **TIP**
❈
To remove the fillets from the fish, see filleting a cooked flat fish, 21. |

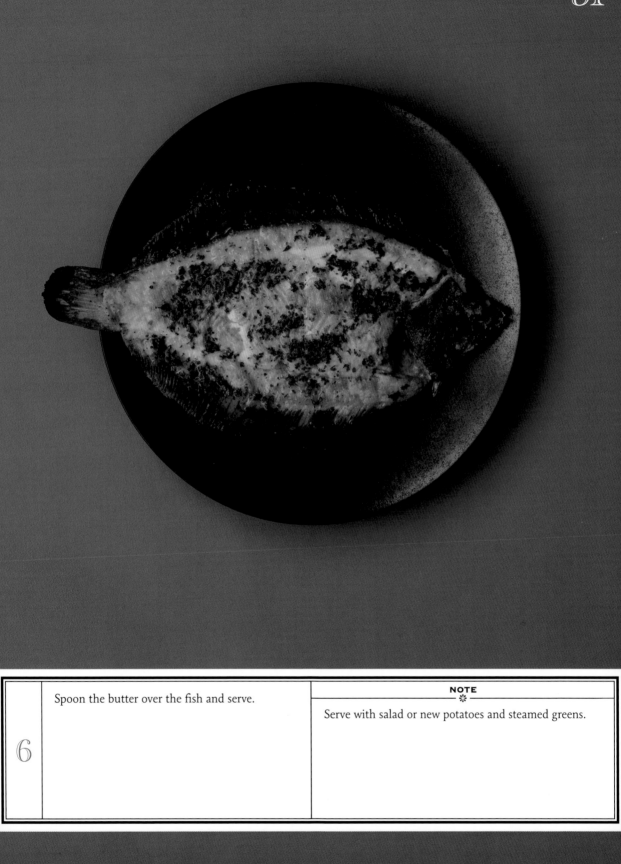

| 6 | Spoon the butter over the fish and serve. | **NOTE**
❄
Serve with salad or new potatoes and steamed greens. |

CRISP CHILI SALT SPRATS

❧ SERVES 4 • PREPARATION : 10 MINUTES • COOKING : 3–4 MINUTES ❧

14 ounce (400 g) sprats
1 cup (200 ml) full fat milk
1 cup (100 g) plain flour
1 tablespoon (15 ml) cayenne pepper
1 teaspoon black pepper

Pinch of salt
2½ cups (600 ml) vegetable oil, for deep-frying

IN ADVANCE :
Heat the oil to 350°F (180°C) in a large heavy-based pan.

1	Place the sprats in a bowl of milk.	2	Mix the flour, cayenne, black pepper and salt together on a plate. Drain the fish and coat with the seasoned flour.
3	Deep-fry the sprats for 3–4 minutes, or until crispy. Remove from the hot oil with a slotted spoon and drain on paper towel.	4	Serve the crispy sprats with parsley, mayonnaise and lemon slices.

FAST FISH

GRILLED FISH

FRIED FISH

ON THE STOVE

EN PAPILLOTE

4

SARDINES WITH SALSA VERDE

❧ SERVES 2 • PREPARATION : 5 MINUTES • COOKING : 6 MINUTES ❧

4 large sardines, heads removed, cleaned and
  gutted

SALSA VERDE :
1 small bunch of parsley, leaves only
½ small bunch of mint, leaves only

½ garlic clove
1 anchovy fillet
1 tablespoon (15 ml) capers
1 teaspoon Dijon mustard
1 teaspoon red wine vinegar
2 tablespoons extra (30 ml) virgin olive oil

Salt and black pepper

IN ADVANCE :
Preheat a grill to high.

1 2
3 4

1	Roughly chop all the ingredients for the salsa verde, put into a bowl and mix together. Season.	2	Score the sardines 2–3 times with a sharp knife.
3	Put some of the salsa into the belly of the fish and a little over the skin of the fish.	4	Put on a tray and cook under the hot grill for 3 minutes on each side. Serve with any remaining salsa verde and lemon wedges.

MACKEREL WITH FETA & MINT

❧ SERVES 2 • PREPARATION : 5–10 MINUTES • COOKING : 6 MINUTES ❧

¼ cup (60 g) feta cheese
1 small bunch of oregano, leaves only
1 red chili, thinly sliced
1 small bunch of mint, stalks removed

1 tablespoon (15 ml) olive oil, plus extra for
  brushing
Salt and black pepper
4 mackerel fillets, skin on and boned
1 fennel, thinly sliced

IN ADVANCE :
Preheat the grill to high.

1	Combine the feta, oregano, chili, mint, 1 tablespoon of oil and seasoning.	2	Put a fillet skin side down on a board and spread the feta mix on top. Repeat.	3	Arrange the fennel on top of the feta.
4	Place the other fillets on top and tie the fillets together with string.	5	Brush the fish with oil, season, grill for 4 minutes, turn and grill for 2 minutes.	6	Once the fish is cooked carefully remove the string and serve with lemon.

HERB-CRUSTED COD

❧ SERVES 2 • PREPARATION : 10 MINUTES • COOKING : 6–10 MINUTES ❧

½ cup (60 g) white breadcrumbs
1 small handful of parsley, chopped
1 tablespoon (15 ml) capers, chopped
zest of ½ a lemon
Salt and black pepper

2 x 7 ounce (200 g) cod fillets, skinned
1 egg, beaten

IN ADVANCE :
Preheat the grill to high.

1 2
3 4

1	Process the breadcrumbs, parsley, capers, lemon zest and seasoning together in a food processor.	2	Dip the fish skin side down into the beaten egg and then coat in the breadcrumb mixture.
3	Place the fish on a tray and grill for about 3–4 minutes on each side.	4	Serve the cod with lemon wedges and salad.

TUNA NIÇOISE

⇨ SERVES 4 • PREPARATION : 10–15 MINUTES • COOKING : 2–3 MINUTES + 5 MINUTES COOLING ⇦

1 tablespoon (15 ml) olive oil, for rubbing
2 x 3½ ounce (100 g) tuna loin steaks
Salt and black pepper
8 ounces (250 g) new potatoes, cooked and
  halved
⅔ cup (100 g) green beans, cooked

⅔ cup (100 g) cherry tomatoes, halved
⅓ cup (50 g) pitted black olives, halved
2 tablespoons (30 g) capers
1 ounce (25 g) anchovy fillets, thinly sliced
2 soft boiled eggs, cut in half
2 small heads lettuce, separated into leaves

DRESSING :
3 tablespoons (45 ml) olive oil
1 tablespoon (15 ml) white wine vinegar
½ teaspoon Dijon mustard
IN ADVANCE :
Heat a griddle pan over high heat.

1	Rub a little oil over the tuna and season.	2	Cook the tuna on the griddle pan for 1 minute each side. Cool for 5 minutes.	3	Mix the potatoes, beans, tomatoes, olives, capers and anchovies together.
4	In another bowl, whisk the ingredients for the dressing and season.	5	Mix the eggs and lettuce with the salad then mix with the dressing; season.	6	Cut the tuna pieces into thin strips, mix into the salad and serve.

FISH TEMPURA

❖ SERVES 2–4 • PREPARATION : 10 MINUTES • COOKING : 2–3 MINUTES ❖

⅔ cup (80 g) plain flour, plus extra for dusting
3 tablespoons (20 g) cornflour, plus extra for dusting
1 teaspoon Chinese five spice
Salt and black pepper
1 egg white

⅔ cup (150 ml) carbonated water
7 ounce (200 g) halibut, skinned and cut into 4 pieces
7 ounce (200 g) haddock, skinned and cut into 4 pieces
5 large shrimp, peeled and butterflied

(see butterflying shrimp , 59)
2 cups (500 ml) sunflower oil
IN ADVANCE :
Heat the oil in a deep-fryer or large heavy-based pan to 350°F (180°C).

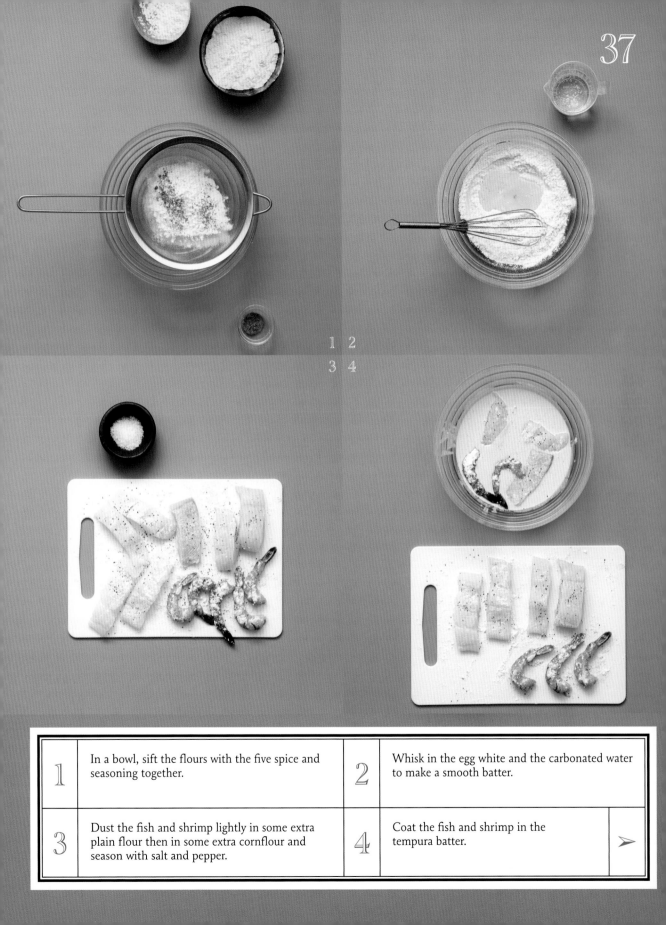

| 1 | In a bowl, sift the flours with the five spice and seasoning together. | 2 | Whisk in the egg white and the carbonated water to make a smooth batter. | |
| 3 | Dust the fish and shrimp lightly in some extra plain flour then in some extra cornflour and season with salt and pepper. | 4 | Coat the fish and shrimp in the tempura batter. | ➤ |

	Deep-fry the fish in the hot oil for about 1–2 minutes, or until golden.	**TIP** ❋	
5		This dish works well with fish with a good texture, such as farmed cod, monkfish and squid rings.	

	VARIATION ✻
6 Remove the tempura with a slotted spoon and drain on paper towel. Serve the tempura with a sprinkle of Chinese five spice powder and lime wedges.	You can also serve the tempura with sweet chili sauce, if you like.

PAN-FRIED SALMON STEAK

❧ SERVES 2 • PREPARATION : 10–15 MINUTES + 10 MINUTES CHILLING • COOKING : 6–8 MINUTES ❧

2 salmon steaks, prepared by the
fishmonger, 2–3 inches (5–8 cm) thick
Salt and black pepper
1 tablespoon (15 ml) olive oil

BUTTER :
1 large bunch of tarragon
½ cup (125 g) butter, softened
2 shallots, finely chopped
1 tablespoon (15 ml) capers, chopped

1 garlic clove, finely chopped

IN ADVANCE :
Heat a frying pan over medium-high heat.

1	For the butter, chop the tarragon, put into a bowl, add the butter, shallots, capers, garlic and seasoning and mix together.	2	Put the butter onto a sheet of parchment paper and roll into a small cylinder. Chill the butter in the refrigerator for 10 minutes.
3	Season the salmon then rub them with the oil. Put in the hot frying pan and cook on each side for 3–4 minutes, or until golden brown.	4	Serve the salmon with some of the tarragon butter and steamed greens.

PAN-FRIED TURBOT

⊱ SERVES 2 • PREPARATION : 10–15 MINUTES • COOKING : 10–12 MINUTES ⊰

1 teaspoon fennel seeds
Pinch of sea salt flakes
1 teaspoon black peppercorns
2 tablespoons (30 ml) olive oil
4 x 10 ounce (300 g) turbot tronçons, filleted
   and sliced, skin on and bone in

¾ cup (100 g) snow peas
¾ cup (100 g) baby corn, halved
1 small bunch of tarragon
3 tablespoons (45 ml) white wine
2 tablespoons (30 g) butter

IN ADVANCE :
Preheat the oven to 450°F (230°C). Cut out
   2 x 15 inch (38 cm) squares of parchment
   paper and aluminum foil. Heat a heavy-
   based frying pan over high heat.

1	Grind the fennel, salt and peppercorns in a pestle and mortar and add the oil.	2	Mix the fish in the herb mixture, turning it over to make sure it is covered.	3	Put the fish, dark skin side down into the hot frying pan and sear for 1 minute.
4	Turn the fish over and sear for a further 1 minute, then leave to one side.	5	Put the snow peas, corn and tarragon on the parchment/foil squares.	6	Put the fish on top with a splash of wine and 2 tablespoons of butter. ➤

| 7 | Close up the bundles and cook in the oven for 8–10 minutes. Remove from the oven and carefully open the bundles, allowing them to cool slightly. | **TIP**
❊
Make sure the fish is completely covered in the herb mixture in step 2. |

| 8 | Remove the fish and vegetables from the bundles and put onto serving plates. Spoon on some of the juices and serve. | **TIP**
※
A tronçon is a steak cut from a large fish. |

GOUJONS OF SOLE WITH AIOLI

❧ SERVES 4 • PREPARATION : 10 MINUTES • COOKING : 2–3 MINUTES ❧

1 pound (500 g) Dover sole, filleted, pin
  boned and skinned
¾ cup (100 g) plain flour
Salt and black pepper
2 eggs, beaten
1 cup (150 g) white breadcrumbs

½ cup (50 g) freshly grated Parmesan
2½ cups (600 ml) vegetable oil

AIOLI :
⅔ cup (200 g) good-quality mayonnaise
½ small garlic clove, finely chopped

Lemon juice, to taste

IN ADVANCE :
Heat the oil for deep-frying in a deep-fryer or
  large heavy-based pan to 375°F (190°C).

1
4

2
5

3
6

1	Cut the sole fillet diagonally into strips about ½ inch (1 cm) thick to make goujons.	2	Put the flour on a plate and season. Coat the goujons in the seasoned flour.	3	Dip the goujons into the beaten eggs.	
4	Mix the breadcrumbs with the cheese and use to coat the fish. Put them on a tray.	5	In a bowl, combine mayonnaise, garlic, lemon juice and seasoning. Set aside.	6	Deep-fry the goujons in the hot oil for 2–3 minutes.	➢

		TIP
7	Remove the goujons with a slotted spoon and drain on paper towel.	Don't overcrowd the fish when frying, otherwise they will stick together – carefully drop 6–8 goujons into the hot oil at a time and deep-fry them until they are golden brown.

| 8 | Serve the goujons with the aioli, some lemon wedges and salad leaves. | **TIP**
❋
Serve the goujons soon after deep-frying otherwise they may lose their crispiness and go soggy. |

PAN-FRIED HERRING ROE

❖ SERVES 2–4 • PREPARATION : 10 MINUTES • COOKING : 5 MINUTES ❖

3 tablespoons (45 ml) plain flour
Salt and black pepper
10 ounces (300 g) herring roe
2 tablespoons (30 g) unsalted butter
1 garlic clove, sliced

1 tablespoon (15 ml) flat leaf parsley, chopped
Juice of ½ lemon

IN ADVANCE :

Heat a heavy-based non-stick frying pan over
 medium heat.

1 2
3 4

1	In a bowl, mix the flour with salt and pepper, then lightly dust the roe with the seasoned flour and put on a plate.	2	Put some of the butter into the hot frying pan, add the roe and fry for 2 minutes, then turn over and fry for a further 2 minutes.
3	Add the remaining butter, the garlic, parsley and lemon juice and cook for a further 1 minute.	4	Place the cod roe on top of an artisanal bread, such as walnut, and serve.

SOLE WITH BUERRE NOISETTE

❧ SERVES 2 • PREPARATION : 10 MINUTES • COOKING : 3–4 MINUTES ❧

2 x 7 ounce (200 g) Dover sole, filleted and
  skinned
3 tablespoons (45 ml) plain flour
Salt and black pepper

¼ cup (60 g) unsalted butter
1 tablespoon (15 ml) olive oil
Juice of ½ lemon
1 tablespoon (15 g) flat leaf parsley, chopped

IN ADVANCE :
Heat a large heavy-based frying pan over
  medium-high heat.

1 2
3 4

1	Dust the fish with flour and seasoning.	2	Melt half of the butter in the hot frying pan, add the oil and fry the fish for 1–2 minutes on each side until lightly browned. Keep warm.
3	Add the rest of the butter to the pan and heat until it is light brown with a nutty smell. Add the lemon juice, parsley and a pinch of salt.	4	Spoon the buerre noisette over the fish and serve.

PAN-FRIED TROUT WITH CAPERS

❖ SERVES 2 • PREPARATION : 5 MINUTES • COOKING : 4–5 MINUTES ❖

1½ tablespoons (20 ml) vegetable oil
5 shallots, thinly sliced
1 small handful of parsley, leaves only
1 tablespoon (15 g) capers, chopped

2 x 5 ounce (150 g) trout fillets, scaled and pin boned
1 tablespoon (15 ml) olive oil
Salt and black pepper

IN ADVANCE :

Heat a heavy-based frying pan over medium-high heat.

1 2
3 4

1	Heat the vegetable oil in a pan and fry the shallots until golden, then drain, put into a bowl with the parsley and capers and mix together.	2	Rub the trout fillets with a little olive oil and season with salt and pepper.
3	Add the trout fillets, skin side down, to the preheated pan and fry for 2 minutes until crispy. Turn over and cook for 30 seconds.	4	Serve the fish skin side up with the capers and shallots and lemon wedges.

STEAMED THAI GRAY MULLET

✦ SERVES 2 • PREPARATION : 5–10 MINUTES • COOKING : 5 MINUTES ✦

2 tablespoons (30 ml) Thai green chili paste
1 teaspoon white peppercorns
2 garlic cloves, sliced
½ cup (50 g) coriander roots, chopped
1 teaspoon caster sugar
1 tablespoon (15 ml) fish sauce

2 tablespoons (30 ml) fresh lime juice
2 large gray mullet fillets, scaled and
pin boned

IN ADVANCE :

Put a steamer on top of a wok of simmering
water, with a lid to cover.

1	Mix the paste, peppercorns, garlic, coriander and sugar with a pestle and mortar.	2	Add the fish sauce and lime juice and stir well.	3	Slash the fish 3 times on each side, then brush the mixture over the fish.
4	Lay the fish in the steamer and put the lid on top.	5	Steam over high heat for 5 minutes, or until cooked.	6	Put the fish in a serving dish and garnish with sliced chili and coriander leaves.

POACHED COD IN OLIVE OIL

✤ SERVES 2–4 • PREPARATION : 5 MINUTES • COOKING : 15 MINUTES ✤

1 white onion, sliced
3 garlic cloves, bashed with the skin on
2–3 whole, long dried red chilies
3 rosemary sprigs
2½ cups (600 ml) olive oil

Salt and black pepper
2 x 8 ounce (250 g) pieces cod, skinned and
    filleted
Good pinch of sea salt, for sprinkling

1	Put the onion, garlic, chilies and rosemary into a large heavy-based pan with the olive oil.	2	Season the cod on both sides and put into the pan. Heat the oil slowly on medium-high heat.
3	Leave the fish to cook for 15 minutes, then carefully lift the fish out of the pan allowing the excess oil to drain off.	4	Put the fish onto a serving plate, sprinkle with salt, garnish with some of the chili, garlic and rosemary pieces from the oil and serve.

QUICK MONKFISH CURRY

❖ SERVES 4 • PREPARATION : 10 MINUTES • COOKING : 18 MINUTES ❖

1 teaspoon black peppercorns
1 tablespoon (15 g) coriander seeds
1 teaspoon cumin seeds
2 tablespoons (30 ml) vegetable oil
1 onion, thinly sliced

3 garlic cloves, thinly sliced
¼ cup (30 g) fresh ginger, grated
1 tablespoon (15 ml) tomato purée
1¾ cups (400 ml) coconut milk
2–3 mild green chilies, finely sliced

Pinch of salt
1 pound (500 g) monkfish, skinned and cut
into thick pieces
3 large handfuls of baby spinach

1	In a spice grinder, grind the peppercorns, coriander and cumin seeds to a powder.	2	Heat the oil in a pan and fry the onion, garlic and ginger for 5 minutes.	3	Stir in the ground spices and cook for a further 2–3 minutes.
4	Add the tomato purée, coconut milk, chilies and salt and simmer for 5 minutes.	5	Gently place the fish into the pan, add the spinach and cook for 5 minutes.	6	Serve the curry with lime wedges and rice, and sprinkled with a little coconut.

ANCHOVY & GARLIC DRESSING

❧ SERVES 2 (AS A SIDE DISH) • PREPARATION : 5 MINUTES • COOKING : 2–3 MINUTES ❧

12 canned anchovy fillets, drained
5 tablespoons (75 ml) extra virgin olive oil
2 garlic cloves, peeled and thinly sliced
Juice of ½ lemon
Salt and black pepper

2 cups (300 g) purple sprouting broccoli or
    regular broccoli

1	Roughly chop the anchovies.	2	Mash the anchovies with the oil, garlic, lemon juice and seasoning with a pestle and mortar.
3	Put the broccoli into a pan of hot water. Add a pinch of salt, cover with a lid and cook for 2–3 minutes. Drain.	4	Serve the broccoli immediately with the dressing spooned over.

FISH EN PAPILLOTE

⤞ SERVES 2 • PREPARATION : 5 MINUTES • COOKING : 5–6 MINUTES ⤝

1 tomato
1 small bunch of basil
2 garlic cloves
¼ cup (50 g) black pitted olives

2 medium-sized sea bass fillets, skin on and pin boned
1 tablespoon (15 ml) olive oil

IN ADVANCE :
Preheat the oven to 350°F (180°C). Prepare the parchment paper and aluminum foil as shown in how to cook en papillote, 06.

1	Chop the tomato, basil, garlic and olives and mix together.	2	Put the basil mix onto the parchment paper, top with the fish and drizzle with a little oil.
3	Close up the paper (see how to cook en papillote, 06), put on a baking tray and bake for 5–6 minutes.	4	Serve the fish and vegetables with a drizzle of extra virgin olive oil. ➤

OTHER VARIATIONS – HAKE

❧ SERVES 1 • PREPARATION : 5 MINUTES • COOKING : 6–8 MINUTES ❧

1 small bunch of parsley
1 garlic clove
10 ounce (300 g) hake fillet, skin on and
pin boned
Salt and black pepper

3 tablespoons (45 ml) white wine
1¼ ounces (50 g) mussels, cleaned and
debearded
2 tablespoons (20 g) butter

IN ADVANCE :
Preheat the oven to 350°F (180°C). Prepare
the parchment paper and aluminum foil as
shown in how to cook en papillote, 06.

1	Chop the parsley and garlic.	2	Put the fish onto the parchment paper and foil, season, then top with the parsley, garlic, wine, mussels and butter.
3	Close up the paper (see how to cook en papillote, 06), put on a baking tray and bake in the oven for 6–8 minutes.	4	Serve with a drizzle of extra virgin olive oil.

OTHER VARIATIONS – RED MULLET

❧ SERVES 1 • PREPARATION : 10 MINUTES • COOKING : 5–6 MINUTES ❧

1 lemongrass
1 red chili
1 small bunch of coriander
1 medium-sized red mullet fillet, skin on and
   pin boned

1 lime, cut in half
Salt and black pepper

IN ADVANCE :

Preheat the oven to 350°F (180°C). Prepare
   the parchment paper and aluminum foil as
   shown in how to cook en papillote, 06.

| 1 | Chop the lemongrass, chili and coriander and mix together. | 2 | Put the fish onto the parchment paper, top with the lemongrass mixture, squeeze over the lime juice and season. |
| 3 | Close up the paper (see how to cook en papillote, 06), put on a baking tray and bake in the oven for 5–6 minutes. | 4 | Serve with the remaining coriander. |

BAKED &
SHALLOW-FRIED FISH

5

SMOKED HADDOCK TART

❧ SERVES 4–6 • PREPARATION : 15 MINUTES • COOKING : 30–35 MINUTES + 15 MINUTES COOLING ❧

14 ounces (400 g) smoked undyed haddock,
   skin on and filleted
1¼ cups (300 ml) milk
1 pound (500 g) baby spinach leaves
3 tablespoons (30 g) butter

8 ounces (250 g) ready-made puff pastry
1 egg yolk, lightly beaten
1 cup (100 g) Emmental cheese, grated
1 teaspoon grated nutmeg
Salt and black pepper

IN ADVANCE :
Preheat the oven to 350°F (180°C).

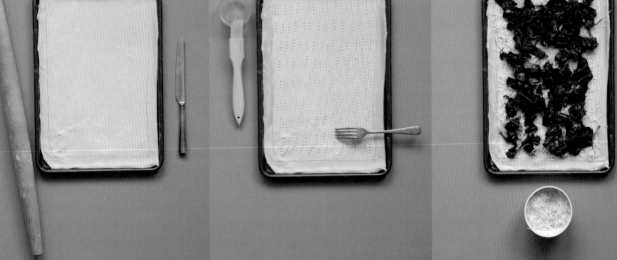

1	Put the fish in a pan with the milk and simmer for 4–5 minutes.	2	Let the fish cool for 10 minutes. Remove skin and flake, removing any bones.	3	Cook the spinach and butter in a pan until slightly wilted. Drain and cool.
4	Roll out pastry to a rectangle, ½ inch (1 cm) thick. Make a border, pinching sides up.	5	Prick holes on the pastry and brush the border with the egg yolk.	6	Sprinkle half the cheese over the base; top with spinach. ➢

| 7 | Put the haddock pieces on top, making sure they are evenly distributed, then scatter the remaining cheese over the top. Sprinkle on the nutmeg, season and bake in the oven for 25–30 minutes. | **TIP**
❀
You may need to cut the haddock in half to fit into the pan in step 1. |

8   Allow the tart to cool slightly then cut into slices and serve.

VARIATION
❋

This tart would also work well with salmon.

SALMON EN CROUTE

➤ SERVES 4–6 • PREPARATION : 10–20 MINUTES + 1 HOUR CHILLING • COOKING : 35–40 MINUTES ⬿

2 x 10 ounce (300 g) pieces salmon fillet,
  skinned and pin boned
1½ pound (750 g) chilled ready rolled puff
  pastry
Plain flour, for dusting
1 egg, beaten, for glaze

BUTTER MIX :
¼ cup (50 g) unsalted butter, softened
½ teaspoon crushed fennel seeds
½ teaspoon mixed black pepper
Grated zest of ½ lemon
1 teaspoon chopped dill

Pinch of salt

IN ADVANCE:
Preheat the oven to 400°F (200°C).

1	Mix all the ingredients for the butter mix together.	2	Spread the mix on the inner face of 1 fillet evenly and put the second fillet on top.	3	Roll the pastry out to a 10 x 14 inch (25 x 35 cm) rectangle then cut into 2 rectangles.	
4	Put 1 rectangle on a tray, put fish in the center and brush egg around the fish.	5	Lay the second pastry piece on top and press tightly around the outside.	6	Trim the edges, press down with a fork, glaze with eggwash and chill.	➤

7	Bake in the oven for 35–40 minutes until golden brown.	**TIP** ❀ Dust the work surface with a little plain flour before rolling out the pastry otherwise the pastry may stick to the surface.

8 | Serve the salmon en croute in slices with steamed asparagus. | **VARIATION** ❊
You can add lots of different flavors to the butter mix, such as basil, parsley or chervil, if you like.

FISH PIZZA

❧ SERVES 4–6 • PREPARATION : 15–20 MINUTES + 1 HOUR RISING • COOKING : 10–12 MINUTES ❧

1 pound (500 g) strong white bread flour
⅛ ounce (5 g) powdered dried yeast
¼ ounce (10 g) salt
1⅓ cups (325ml) warm water
About 1 tablespoon (15 ml) olive oil, plus extra for cooking and drizzling

Plain flour, for dusting
1 garlic clove, sliced
1 x 14 ounce (400 g) can chopped tomatoes
Pinch of dried chili flakes
5 ounce (150 g) salmon, cooked and broken into pieces

3½ ounces (100 g) black pepper mackerel, cooked and broken into pieces
3½ ounces (100 g) shrimp, cooked
IN ADVANCE :
Preheat the oven to 425°F (220°C). Put a baking sheet in to heat.

1	Mix the flour, yeast, salt and water to form a dough. Mix in the oil, turn out onto a surface and knead until smooth. Shape into a ball.	2	Cover with a plastic bag and leave in a warm area until doubled in size. Roll out the dough into a large rectangle.	
3	Put a little oil, the garlic, tomatoes and chili into a pan and cook for about 5 minutes.	4	Spread the tomato mixture on top of the dough.	➤

		TIP
5	Add the fish and shrimp, drizzle over some olive oil and bake in the oven for about 10–12 minutes, or until cooked.	Dust the work surface with a little plain flour before rolling out the dough, otherwise it may stick to the surface. After rolling the dough out to a large rectangle, transfer it to a large lightly floured baking tray.

Serve the pizza with oil and a little arugula.	**VARIATION** ❄
6	Top the pizza with some of the hot smoked salmon (see hot smoked salmon, 12).

FISH PIE

❧ SERVES 6–8 • PREPARATION : 15 MINUTES • COOKING : 35–40 MINUTES ❧

1 small bunch of dill, finely chopped
1 large bunch of green onions, chopped
12 ounce (350 g) smoked haddock, skinned
1 pound (500 g) pollack fillets, skinned
7 ounce (200 g) salmon fillets, skinned
7 ounce (200 g) raw shrimp, peeled

1 large lemon
Olive oil, for drizzling
2 tablespoons (30 g) capers
Salt and black pepper
¼ cup (50 g) unsalted butter, melted
⅔ cup (75 g) plain flour

3 cups (750 ml) milk
2 teaspoons Dijon mustard
2 pounds (1 kg) potatoes, cooked and mashed
¼ cup (50 g) butter, cut into small cubes
IN ADVANCE :
Preheat the oven to 400°F (200°C).

1	Put the dill and green onions in a large baking dish.	2	Cut the fish into bite-sized chunks and add to the dish with the shrimp.	3	Squeeze over the lemon, drizzle with oil, add capers and seasoning; mix.
4	Mix melted butter with the flour. Slowly stir in the milk until it begins to thicken.	5	Remove from the heat, season and stir in the mustard. Pour over the fish.	6	Spread the mashed potatoes over the top of the fish. ➤

| 7 | Dot some small squares of butter over the top of the pie and bake in the oven for about 35–40 minutes, or until cooked through, crispy and golden on top. | **TIP**
❈
To make the mashed potato topping, cook 2 pounds (1 kg) potatoes, then drain and mash them. Add ¼ cup (50 g) butter, ½ cup (100 ml) double cream, a large pinch of grated nutmeg, a good pinch of salt and pepper and mix well. |

8 | Serve the fish pie with some minted fresh peas.

TIP
❋

Use undyed smoked haddock for the dish.

SMOKED HADDOCK FISH CAKES

❧ SERVES 4–6 • PREPARATION : 20 MINUTES + 25–30 MINUTES CHILLING • COOKING : 15–20 MINUTES ❧

1¼ pound (600 g) smoked undyed haddock,
   skin on, pin boned and cut in half
2 cups (500 ml) milk
2 bay leaves
½ teaspoon black peppercorns
1 tablespoon (15 ml) chopped chives

1 teaspoon chopped parsley
8 ounce (250 g) potatoes, cooked and mashed
2 boiled eggs, shelled and chopped
Salt and black pepper
½ cup (50 g) plain flour, for dusting
2 eggs, beaten

1 cup (150 g) breadcrumbs
2 tablespoons sunflower oil, for frying

IN ADVANCE:
Preheat oven to 350°F (180°C). Heat the oil
   in a frying pan over medium heat.

1	Cook the haddock, milk, bay and peppercorns gently for 5–8 minutes. Drain.	2	Flake the fish with a fork. Remove the skin and ensure there are no bones.	3	Add the herbs, potatoes, eggs and seasoning. Chill until the mix is firm.
4	Shape the mixture into small cakes, dusting them with flour.	5	Dip the fish cakes into the beaten eggs.	6	Coat the fish cakes completely in the breadcrumbs. ➤

| 7 | Fry the cakes in batches in the hot oil for about 3–4 minutes on each side until golden and crispy. Remove the cakes from the pan with a slotted spoon and drain on paper towel. Put the cakes on a baking tray and bake in the oven for a further 5 minutes. | **TIP** ❊

 Allow the fish cakes to drain on paper towel to remove the excess oil before baking them in the oven. |

8

Serve the fish cakes right away with lemon wedges.

TIP
❋

You can also make these cakes with pike, cod, gurnard or black bream.

SALT COD FRITTERS

❧ SERVES 6 • PREPARATION : 20 MINUTES + OVERNIGHT SOAKING • COOKING : 1 HOUR + 5–10 MINUTES COOLING ❧

1 pound (500 g) dried salt cod fillets (see tip)
3 small bay leaves
2 tablespoons (30 ml) olive oil
½ cup (50 g) plain flour
3 medium eggs
7 ounces (200 g) potatoes, cooked and put
   through a ricer

2 garlic cloves, crushed
1 tablespoon (15 ml) chopped flat leaf parsley
1 roasted red pepper, diced
Salt and black pepper
⅔ cup (150 ml) vegetable oil, for frying

IN ADVANCE :
Please see tip for preparation of salt cod.
Heat the oil in a pan over high heat.

1 2
3 4

1	Put the salt cod and bay leaves into a pan and cover with water. Bring just to below boiling point over medium heat for 4–5 minutes.	2	Allow the fish to cool for 5–10 minutes, then remove the skin and any bones and flake the flesh with a fork.
3	Heat 1¼ cups (300 ml) water with the oil to boiling point, take off heat and slowly beat in flour to form a batter. Cool slightly.	4	Beat the eggs into the batter, one at a time. ➤

5 6
7 8

5	Put the mashed potato in a large bowl and mix in the salt cod, garlic, parsley, red pepper and seasoning to taste.	6	Mix the salt cod mixture into the batter.
7	In a large non-stick pan, cook the mixture over low heat for 10 minutes, stirring, until the mixture thickens. Cool slightly.	8	Form the mixture into 15–20 small balls. Put the balls, in batches of 5–6 at a time, into the hot oil and fry until golden brown.

| 9 | Remove the fritters from the pan with a slotted spoon and drain on paper towel. Serve hot with tomato chutney and lemon wedges. | **TIP** ❉

Before cooking the salt cod rinse the excess salt off the cod, then put into a bowl of cold water. Make sure it is submerged then leave to soak in the refrigerator for 24 hours, changing the water 3–4 times a day. |

SEAFOOD STARTERS

6

COOKING & PREPARING CRAB

1	Cook the crab in boiling water for 15 minutes. Allow to cool.	2	Break off the crab claws, legs and tail flap.	3	Push blade between body and back shell and twist the blade to release it.
4	Put thumbs on either side of body and press firmly until it comes away.	5	Pull feather gills away (dead man's fingers) and discard.	6	Scoop out brown meat from the center. Cut it in half.

7	Remove the white crab meat from all of the little channels with a crab pick.	8	Crack the claws and remove the white meat. Discard the thin piece of bone.	9	Remove the crab meat from the small claws with a mallet to break the claws.
10	Press down on the shell behind the eye and discard mouth and stomach.	11	Scoop out any brown meat with a spoon.	12	You should be left with separate bowls of white and brown meat to use.

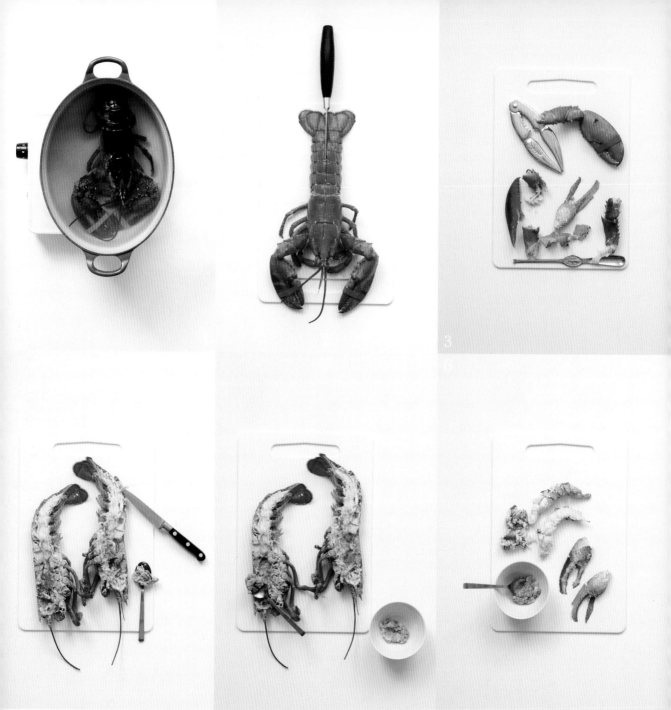

COOKING & PREPARING LOBSTER

1	Freeze lobster for 2 hours. Cook in boiling salted water for 15 minutes; cool.	2	Put the lobster belly-side down on the board and cut in half lengthwise.	3	Break off the claws, bash and remove the claw meat, and put on a plate.
4	Pull out the stomach sac and discard.	5	Remove the soft green tomalley (liver) and red roe from the head section.	6	Remove the meat from the tail and put all of the lobster meat onto the board.

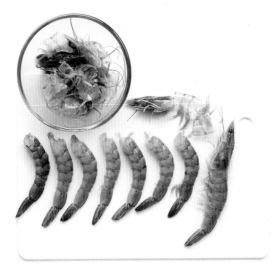

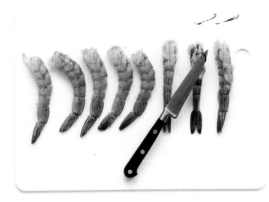

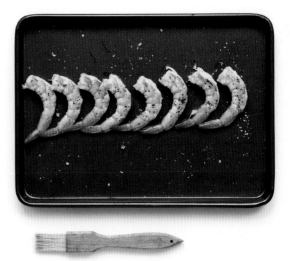

BUTTERFLYING SHRIMP

1	Peel the shrimp, optionally leaving the tail part on or off.	2	Make a deep cut down the back of each shrimp.
3	Pull out the intestinal vein if dark and visible. It is not essential and it doesn't affect the taste.	4	Brush with oil, season, then cook under a hot grill for 2–3 minutes. Serve with lemon.

HARISSA SHRIMP

❧ SERVES 2 • PREPARATION : 5 MINUTES • COOKING : 6–8 MINUTES ❧

12 large jumbo shrimp
3½ ounces (100 g) haloumi cheese, cut into pieces
2 tablespoons (30 ml) harissa chili paste

IN ADVANCE :

Soak 4 wooden skewers in a bowl of water for 30 minutes. Heat a barbecue or a chargrill pan over high heat.

1 2
3 4

1	Peel the shrimp and leave the tail part intact.	2	In a small bowl, mix the shrimp and haloumi with the harissa. Thread onto the skewers with the haloumi placed between the prawns.
3	Chargrill or barbecue the skewers for about 3–4 minutes on each side, or until the shrimp are cooked through.	4	Serve the shrimp on the skewers with flat bread, lemon wedges and hummus.

SHRIMP WRAPPED IN NOODLES

⬦ SERVES 2–4 • PREPARATION : 20 MINUTES • COOKING : 2–3 MINUTES ⬦

10 large jumbo shrimp, butterflied (see butterflying shrimp, 59), with tail on
1 tablespoon (15 ml) Japanese spice powder or chili powder
3½ ounces (100 g) thin fresh egg noodles

1¼ cups (400 ml) vegetable oil, for deep-frying
Salt and black pepper

IN ADVANCE :
Heat the oil in a deep-fryer or a large heavy-based pan to 350°F (180°C).

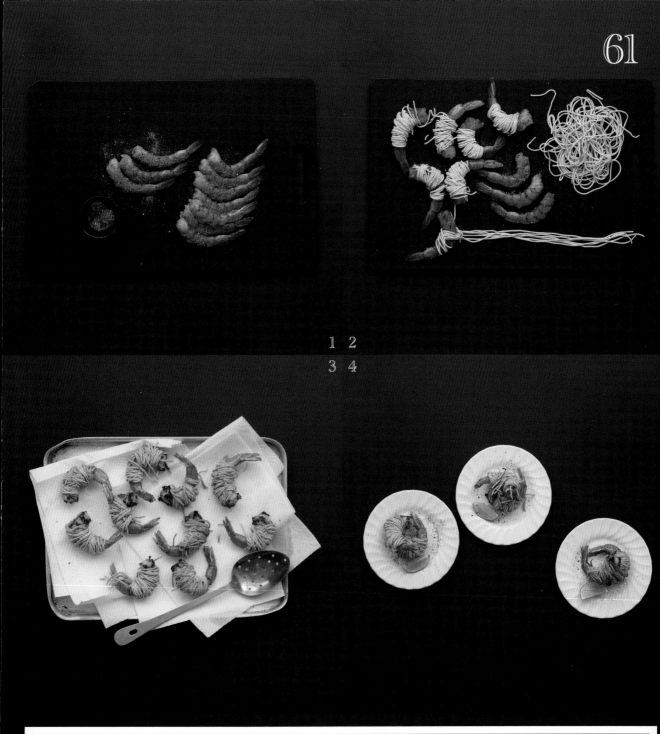

1	Sprinkle the shrimp with the Japanese spice powder or chili powder.	2	Wrap the noodles around the shrimp.
3	Deep-fry the shrimp in the hot oil for 2–3 minutes, or until golden. Remove with a slotted spoon and drain on paper towel. Season.	4	Serve the noodle shrimp warm with lime wedges and Japanese spice powder or chili powder sprinkled over.

VIETNAMESE SHRIMP ROLLS

❖ SERVES 2–4 • PREPARATION : 5–10 MINUTES • COOKING : NIL ❖

7 ounces (200 g) cooked small shrimp
⅔ cup (70 g) Chinese white cabbage, shredded
½ teaspoon chili sauce
1 tablespoon (15 ml) fish sauce
1 tablespoon (15 ml) ginger, finely grated
2 tablespoons (30 g) mint leaves

2 tablespoons (30 g) coriander leaves
1 lime, halved
1 packet round Vietnamese rice papers

TIP :
If rice papers are unavailable, steamed iceberg
lettuce leaves also work well in this dish.

1 2
3 4

1	Combine all of the ingredients together, except the lime and rice papers. Squeeze in the lime juice and mix well.	2	Soak the rice papers in a shallow dish until soft, then separate out carefully.
3	Place 2–3 tablespoons (30–45 ml) of the mix into the center of each rice paper and fold over side flaps. Fold over the bottom flap and roll it tightly.	4	Serve with chili sauce, lime wedges, coriander leaves and sliced red chili. Cut in half to serve.

POTTED BROWN SHRIMP

❧ SERVES 5 • PREPARATION : 5–10 MINUTES • COOKING : 1–2 MINUTES + 1 HOUR CHILLING ❧

½ cup (100 g) butter
Pinch of cayenne pepper
10 ounces (300 g) brown shrimp, cooked
1 small bunch of chives, chopped
Salt and black pepper

TIP :
Best eaten on the day but can be stored in the refrigerator for 2–3 days. Any fresh herbs of your choice could also be used such as dill, parsley and tarragon.

1	Put the butter and cayenne pepper into a pan and gently heat until the butter is melted.	2	Add the shrimp and chives to the pan and warm until the mixture has heated through. Make sure it doesn't boil. Season well.
3	Remove from the heat and divide the mixture into 5 ramekins. Cover and leave to set in the refrigerator for 1 hour.	4	Remove from the refrigerator and allow to stand for a few minutes before serving. Serve with toasted soda bread and lemon wedges.

CHILI SALT SQUID

✣ SERVES 2 • PREPARATION : 5–10 MINUTES • COOKING : 2–3 MINUTES ✣

8 ounces (250 g) squid, cleaned with tentacles
⅔ cup (150 ml) whole milk
½ cup (50 g) plain flour
½ teaspoon salt
Pinch of black pepper

2 tablespoons (30 g) cayenne pepper
2 cups (500 ml) vegetable oil, for deep-frying

IN ADVANCE :

Heat the oil in a deep-fryer or large heavy-based pan to 375°F (190°C).

1 2
3 4

1	Slice the squid into strips, trim the tentacles then dip them into milk.	2	Season the flour with the salt, black pepper and cayenne, then put the squid into the seasoned flour to coat and shake off any excess.
3	Deep-fry the squid in the hot oil for 2–3 minutes until golden brown. Remove with a slotted spoon and drain on paper towel.	4	Serve immediately with lemon wedges, sliced green onions and sliced red chili.

STUFFED BAKED SQUID

✦ SERVES 2–4 • PREPARATION : 10 MINUTES • COOKING : 35–40 MINUTES ✦

4 medium-sized squid, cleaned with tentacles
¾ cup (100 g) toasted breadcrumbs
1 tablespoon (15 ml) capers, chopped
3 garlic cloves, sliced
8 tinned anchovy fillets, chopped
1 tablespoon (15 ml) chopped flat-leaf parsley

4 tablespoons (60 ml) olive oil
Salt and black pepper
14 ounce (400 g) can chopped tomatoes

IN ADVANCE :
Preheat the oven to 350°F (180°C).

1	Chop the squid tentacles into small pieces.	2	In a bowl, mix together the breadcrumbs with the capers, garlic, anchovies, parsley, squid tentacles, 3 tablespoons (45 ml) oil and seasoning.
3	Put a little of this stuffing mixture into each of the squid, and secure the ends with cocktail sticks.	4	Put the remaining oil in a pan and cook the stuffed squid for 1 minute. ➢

5   Add the tomatoes to the pan, then season. Transfer to the oven and bake for 35–40 minutes, or until tender.

TIP
❋

Be sure to use an ovenproof frying pan as the squid is finished in the oven. If you don't have one, then carefully transfer the contents of the pan to an ovenproof baking dish.

| 6 | Sprinkle some more chopped parsley over the squid, then season to taste and serve. | **NOTE**
❀
Serve the squid with salad leaves and warm crusty bread for a delicious summer lunch. |

CRUMBED LANGOUSTINES

❖ SERVES 2 • PREPARATION : 5 MINUTES • COOKING : 4–5 MINUTES + 5–10 MINUTES COOLING ❖

12 langoustines, fresh if available
½ cup (100 ml) white wine
⅓ cup (50 g) breadcrumbs
1 ounce (30 g) finely chopped pancetta
1 tablespoon (15 g) chopped parsley
Salt and black pepper

IN ADVANCE :
Preheat the grill to high.
If the langoustines are frozen, defrost them
  completely before cooking them.

1 2
3 4

1	Heat a large frying pan until hot, then add the langoustines with the wine, cover and cook for 2 minutes. Allow to cool slightly.	2	Put the cooled langoustines belly-side down on a board and cut in half lengthwise .	
3	Remove the creamy contents of the langoustines' head and put into a bowl.	4	Add the breadcrumbs, pancetta, parsley and seasoning to the bowl and mix together.	➤

| 5 | Put the langoustine halves on a baking tray and top with the crumb mixture. Cook under the grill for 1–2 minutes, or until golden. | **TIP**
❋
Use fresh white breadcrumbs for the stuff |

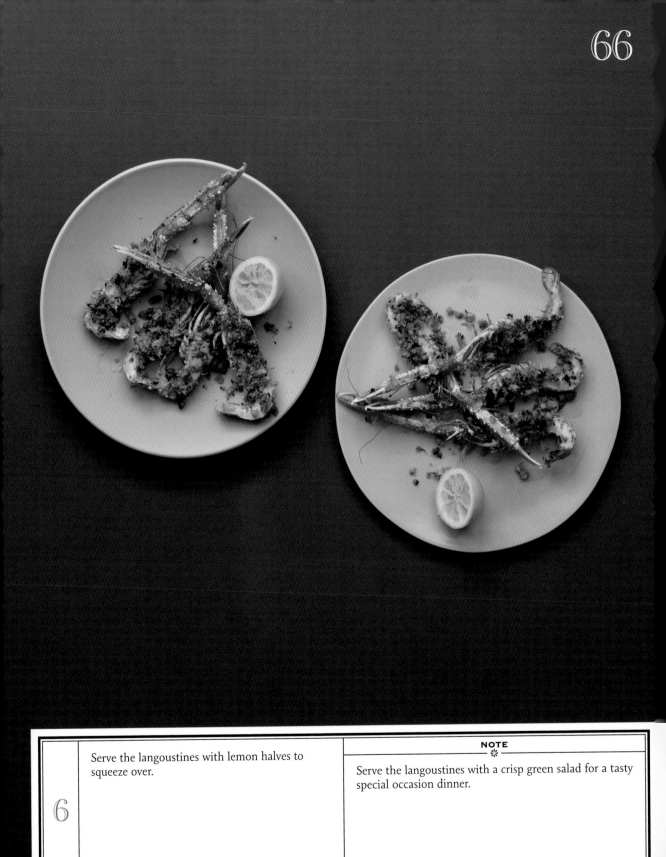

6

Serve the langoustines with lemon halves to squeeze over.

NOTE

Serve the langoustines with a crisp green salad for a tasty special occasion dinner.

ISPY SOFT-SHELLED CRA

SERVES 4 (AS A STARTER) • PREPARATION : 5 MINUTES • COOKING : 2–3 MINUTES

s, cleaned
n flour
lour
...
l) ground black pepper

½ cup (100 ml) soda water
2 cups (500 ml) vegetable oil, for deep-frying

IN ADVANCE :
Heat the oil in a deep-fryer or large heavy-
based pan to 375°F (190°C).

NOTE :
Check with your fishmon
man's fingers underneat
have been removed, see
crab, 57.

1 2
3 4

1	Cut the crabs in half with a sharp knife.	2	Mix the flours, paprika, black pepper, a squeeze of lemon and the soda water together in a bowl. Dip the crabs into the batter.
3	Deep-fry the crabs in the hot oil for about 2–3 minutes, or until golden. Remove with a slotted spoon and drain on paper towel.	4	Serve with lime wedges and chili sauce.

CARPET SHELL CLAMS IN BEER

❖ SERVES 2 • PREPARATION : 5–10 MINUTES • COOKING : 4–5 MINUTES ❖

1 tablespoon (15 ml) vegetable oil
1 bunch of green onions, sliced
1 garlic clove, sliced
Pinch of dried chili flakes
2 pounds (900 g) clams, washed

2 tablespoons (30 g) butter
Salt and black pepper
1 cup (200 ml) dark beer/stout

NOTE :
Discard any clams that have not opened after cooking.

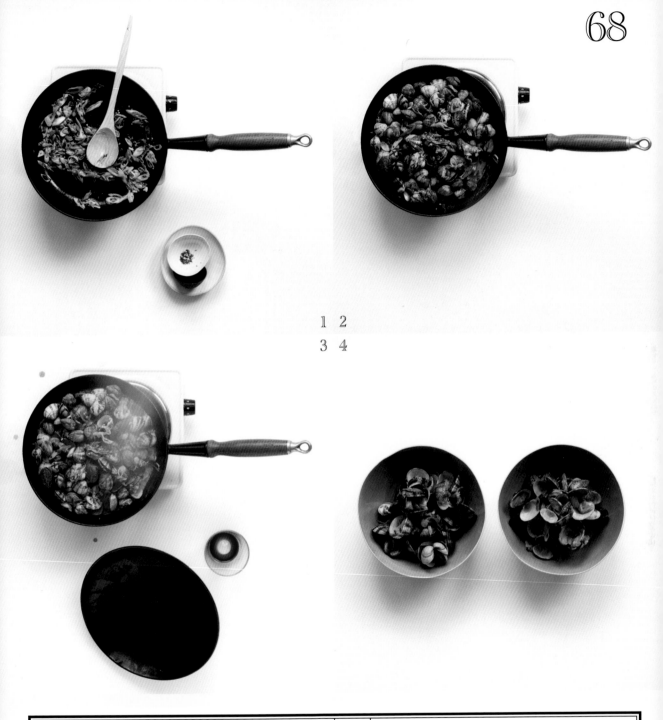

1 2
3 4

1	Heat the oil in a frying pan and cook the green onions, garlic and chili flakes for 1 minute, or until fragrant.	2	Add the clams and butter to the pan and gently cook for about 1–2 minutes. Season.
3	Add the beer/stout, cover and cook over high heat, giving the pan a good shake occasionally until all the clams have opened.	4	Put the clams into warmed serving bowls and spoon over the juices. Serve with crusty bread.

MUSSELS WITH CHORIZO CRUMB

➤ SERVES 4 • PREPARATION : 5 MINUTES • COOKING : 5–6 MINUTES + 5–10 MINUTES COOLING ◆

36 large mussels scrubbed and debearded
½ cup (100 ml) dry white wine
3½ ounces (100 g) fresh white bread
½ bunch of parsley, leaves only
1¾ ounces (50 g) chorizo sausage, chopped

2 tablespoons (30 ml) olive oil

IN ADVANCE :
Heat a pan over high heat. Preheat the grill
to high.

1 2
3 4

1	Put the mussels and wine into the hot pan. Cover with a lid and cook for 3–4 minutes, or until the mussels have opened. Allow to cool.	2	Once the mussels are cool enough to handle strain the liquid and discard the empty half shells and any unopened mussels.	
3	Lay the cooked mussels on a tray.	4	Put the bread, parsley and chorizo in a food processor and blend to make crumbs.	➤

| 5 | Top the mussels with the crumb mixture and drizzle with the oil. Cook the mussels under the hot grill for 2 minutes, or until golden. | **TIP**
❀
Use a heavy-based frying or a heavy-based casserole pan to cook the mussels in step 1, but make sure the pan has a tight-fitting lid. |

	Serve the mussels immediately.	**NOTES** ❋
6		Use a teaspoon to put the chorizo crumb mixture carefully onto the mussel halves in step 5. If you like, serve the mussels with a green salad.

RAZOR CLAMS IN GARLIC

❖ SERVES 2 • PREPARATION : 5–10 MINUTES • COOKING : 4–5 MINUTES ❖

1 tablespoon (15 ml) vegetable oil
8 razor clams, scrubbed
2 garlic cloves, finely sliced
3 tablespoons (20 g) butter
½ cup (50 g) flat leaf parsley, chopped

NOTE :
Razor clams are also called razor fish. Before using, scrub them thoroughly under cold running water.

1	Heat a large heavy-based pan, add the oil, increase the heat to high, then when the pan is very hot, add the clams.	2	As soon as the clams begin to open turn them over so the meat touches the pan. Reduce the heat, stir in the garlic and cook for 1 minute.
3	Turn the clams over, then add the butter and chopped parsley. Discard any clams that are still closed.	4	Serve the clams with the juices from the pan.

BEER-BATTERED OYSTERS

❧ SERVES 2 • PREPARATION : 5–10 MINUTES • COOKING : 1 MINUTE ❧

12 oysters, shelled
2 cups (500 ml) vegetable oil for deep-frying

BEER BATTER :
½ cup (50 g) plain flour
½ cup (50 g) cornflour, sifted
Good pinch of sea salt
½ cup (100 ml) light beer or soda water, chilled

IN ADVANCE :
Heat the oil in a deep-fryer or a large heavy-based pan to 375°F (190°C). To open the oysters, see oysters with tarragon, 72.

1	For the batter, put the flours and salt into a large bowl and pour in the light beer, a little at a time, until it comes together.	2	Dip the oysters into the batter making sure that they are evenly coated.
3	Deep-fry the oysters in the hot oil for about 1 minute, then remove with a slotted spoon and drain on paper towel.	4	Serve the oysters with a sweet chili dipping sauce and lime wedges.

OYSTERS WITH TARRAGON

❧ SERVES 2 • PREPARATION : 5–10 MINUTES • COOKING : NIL ❧

6 native oysters
2 tarragon sprigs
¼ cup (50 ml) red wine vinegar
1 shallot, finely chopped

1 2
3 4

1	Put a thick cloth underneath the oyster. Using an oyster knife push it into the hinge located at the narrowest point.	2	Work the knife back and forth until it opens. Remove the ligament joint and loosen the oyster from the shell.
3	Chop the tarragon and mix together with the red wine vinegar and shallot.	4	Spoon the red wine vinegar mixture over the opened oysters and serve on crushed ice.

SCALLOPS WITH MUSHROOMS

✦ SERVES 2 • PREPARATION : 5 MINUTES • COOKING : 3–5 MINUTES ✦

4 bay scallops, cleaned and trimmed
Salt and black pepper
1 teaspoon finely grated ginger
4 clean scallop shells
1 tablespoon (15 ml) sesame oil

1 tablespoon (15 ml) soy sauce
8 shiitake mushrooms, sliced
3 green onions, finely chopped

IN ADVANCE :
Put a steamer over a pan of simmering water.

1	For the scallops, season them and sprinkle with the grated ginger.	2	Transfer the scallops to the scallop shells, then put them into the steamer, cover with the lid and cook for about 2–3 minutes.
3	Put the sesame oil and soy sauce in a pan and warm through, add the mushrooms and gently fry for 1–2 minutes. Add the green onions.	4	Serve the scallops with the mushrooms and the juices poured over.

SCALLOPS WITH PROSCIUTTO

➤ SERVES 2 • PREPARATION : 5–10 MINUTES • COOKING : 4–5 MINUTES ➤

4 slices prosciutto
3 tablespoons (20 g) butter
1 tablespoon (15 ml) olive oil
8 large scallops, cleaned

Salt and black pepper
3 tablespoons (45 ml) white wine vinegar
1 tablespoon (15 ml) chopped parsley

NOTE :
Once the scallops are cooked in step 2, remove
them from the pan, cover and keep warm,
but keep the juices in the pan.

1	Fry the prosciutto in a frying pan until crispy, then drain on paper towel.	2	In a non-stick pan, melt the butter and oil and heat over high heat. Add the scallops, season and fry for 2 minutes on each side. Keep warm.
3	Return the pan to the heat, pour in the white wine vinegar and mix with the juices from the scallops. Add the parsley.	4	Put the prosciutto on warmed plates, top with the scallops and pour the sauce over.

SEAFOOD MAIN COURSES

7

CLASSIC

GRILLED & BAKED

STEAMED & FRIED

SPANISH SEAFOOD PAELLA

⇜ SERVES 4–6 • PREPARATION : 10–15 MINUTES • COOKING : 20–25 MINUTES ⇝

2 tablespoons (30 ml) olive oil
8 large shrimp, raw
7 ounces (200 g) thickly sliced chorizo sausage
2 garlic cloves, sliced
1 white onion, chopped
3½ ounces (100 g) baby squid, cut into rings

2 tomatoes, roughly chopped
2 cups (400 g) short grain or paella rice
Good pinch of saffron strands
4 cups (1 L) fish stock
8 ounces (250 g) mussels, cleaned and
  debearded

Salt and black pepper

1 2
3 4

1	Heat the oil in a pan and gently cook the shrimp for 2–3 minutes. Remove and set aside.	2	Add the chorizo sausage, garlic and onion to the pan and brown for 1–2 minutes.	
3	Add the squid, tomatoes and rice and cook for 2 minutes.	4	Stir in the saffron and stock and bring to a boil. Reduce the heat to low and simmer for a further 10–15 minutes.	➤

5

Add the mussels and shrimp to the rice and cook for 4–5 minutes, or until the mussels open. Check the seasoning.

TIP

❋

Discard any mussels that are still closed after cooking.

6 | Sprinkle on some chopped parsley and serve.

VARIATION
❀

You can use langoustines instead of shrimp.

CREAMY SEAFOOD RISOTTO

➤ SERVES 4 • PREPARATION : 10–15 MINUTES • COOKING : 25–30 MINUTES ➤

14 ounces (400 g) seafood; i.e. 6 shrimp, 7 ounces (200 g) clams and 7 ounces (200 g) mussels
4 cups (1 L) fish stock
¼ cup (50 g) butter

2 shallots, finely chopped
1 celery stick, chopped
2 garlic cloves, chopped
1⅔ cups (350 g) risotto rice
¾ cup (150 ml) dry white wine

⅔ cup (60 g) Parmesan cheese, grated
Salt and black pepper
Extra virgin olive oil, for drizzling

1	Peel the shrimp and set the shells aside.	2	Heat the stock and shrimp shells in a pan and reduce; keep at a gentle simmer.	3	Melt two-thirds of the butter and cook the shallots, celery and garlic until soft.
4	Add the rice to the shallots and coat in butter. Add wine; cook for 5–6 minutes.	5	Add a ladleful of the simmering stock to the risotto and stir until it is absorbed.	6	Stir in stock, a ladleful at a time. Stir for 15–20 minutes. ➣

| 7 | Add all the seafood to the pan and cook for 2–3 minutes, or until the seafood is cooked. | **TIP**
❋
When adding the stock in step 6, add a ladleful at a time and wait until it is absorbed before adding another. When all the stock has been used the rice should be creamy but al dente. This should take about 20 minutes. |

| 8 | Mix in a little grated Parmesan and the remaining butter, then season to taste with salt and pepper and drizzle with a little extra virgin olive oil. Sprinkle with some more grated Parmesan and serve immediately. | **NOTE**
❋
Serve the risotto with lemon wedges and arugula, if you like. |

MOULES MARINIÈRE

❧ SERVES 2–3 • PREPARATION : 5–10 MINUTES • COOKING : 10 MINUTES ❧

2 tablespoons (30 g) butter
1 onion, chopped
1 garlic clove, sliced
1¼ cups (300 ml) white wine
2 pounds (1 kg) mussels, cleaned and
  debearded

¾ cup plus 2 tablespoons (150 ml) heavy
  cream
Sea salt and black pepper

1	Melt the butter in a large heavy-based pot and gently cook the onion and garlic until the onion is softened.	2	Pour in the wine and bring to a boil.	
3	Add the mussels to the pot, cover and simmer for 2–3 minutes, or until the mussels have opened.	4	Remove the mussels with a slotted spoon and discard any that remain closed.	➤

5	Return the pot to the burner. Add the cream, season to taste and allow the mixture to reduce. Return the mussels to the pot.	**TIP** ❋ Make sure when cooking the mussels in step 3 to use a tight-fitting lid and shake the pot occasionally during cooking until the mussels open.

| 6 | Serve the mussels in warmed bowls with a sprinkling of chopped parsley over the top. | **NOTE**
❈
This dish is good served with some warm crusty bread. |

MARYLAND CRAB CAKES

❖ SERVES 3 • PREPARATION : 10–15 MINUTES + 1 HOUR CHILLING • COOKING : 4–6 MINUTES ❖

12 ounces (350 g) fresh crabmeat
1¼ ounces (40 g) cream crackers, broken into
  crumbs
1 tablespoon (15 ml) Dijon mustard
1 tablespoon (15 ml) lemon juice

Salt and black pepper
1 egg
2 tablespoons (30 ml) chopped parsley
1 tablespoon (15 ml) oil, for frying

1	Put the crabmeat into a bowl with the crushed crackers and allow the crackers to absorb the moisture from the crabmeat.	2	In another bowl, mix the mustard, lemon juice and seasoning together.
3	Beat the egg into the crabmeat, then stir in the parsley and lemon juice mixture and season.	4	Divide the crabmeat into 6 round cakes, about 3 inches (8 cm) in diameter. Cover in cling wrap and chill for 1 hour. ➤

| 5 | Heat a little oil in a large frying pan and fry the crab cakes gently for 2–3 minutes on each side, or until golden. | **TIP** ❋

Use your hands to divide and shape the mixture into crab cakes. |

6	Serve the crab cakes with a fresh green salad and lemon wedges.	**VARIATION** ❋
		You can also serve these crab cakes with tartar sauce and lemon wedges.

LOBSTER THERMIDOR

❖ SERVES 2 • PREPARATION : 5–10 MINUTES • COOKING : 6–10 MINUTES ❖

1 cooked lobster, cut in half lengthwise (see cooking & preparing lobster, 58, and tip) with the shell
2 tablespoons (30 ml) butter
2 shallots, finely chopped

1¼ cups (300 ml) fish stock
4 tablespoons (60 ml) Cognac
½ cup (100 ml) heavy cream
1 tablespoon (15 ml) lemon juice
1 teaspoon English mustard

Salt and black pepper
2 tablespoons (30 ml) grated Parmesan cheese

IN ADVANCE :
Preheat the grill to high.

1	Scoop out the meat from the lobster and cut into large pieces.	2	Put the meat back into the cleaned shell sides, cover and set aside.
3	Melt the butter in a pan and gently fry the shallots for 2–3 minutes until softened. Pour in the fish stock and Cognac.	4	Add the cream, lemon juice and mustard to the pan, then season to taste and allow it to reduce by half. ➤

| 5 | Put the lobster on a baking tray, spoon the sauce over the lobster and sprinkle with the Parmesan. Cook under the grill for 2–3 minutes, or until light golden brown. | **VARIATION**
✳
Use a pinch of paprika instead of the black pepper, if you like. |

	Serve immediately with a watercress salad.	**TIP** ✳
6		Make sure the grill is very hot before cooking.

CREAMED CLAM LINGUINE

❧ SERVES 2 • PREPARATION : 5–10 MINUTES • COOKING : 6–7 MINUTES ❧

10 ounces (300 g) small clams, washed
3 garlic cloves, sliced
½ cup (125 ml) white wine
8 ounces (250 g) linguine, cooked according to
   packet instructions

½ cup (100 g) crème fraîche
Salt and black pepper

PANGRETTA :
½ cup (60 g) breadcrumbs
Grated zest of 1 lemon
1 red chili, thinly sliced
1 bunch of parsley, chopped

1	In a large pan, put the clams, garlic and white wine and cook for 1–2 minutes.	2	To make the pangretta, put the breadcrumbs, lemon zest, chili and parsley in a separate pan and cook until golden. Set aside.
3	Add the cooked pasta and crème fraîche to the clams, season and warm through. Discard any clams that have not opened.	4	Serve the pasta and clams with the pangretta on top.

RISOTTO NERO

⊱ SERVES 4 • PREPARATION : 10–15 MINUTES • COOKING : 20–25 MINUTES ⊰

4 packets of squid ink
5 cups (1.2 L) fish stock
¼ cup (50 g) butter
3 shallots, finely chopped
1 garlic clove, chopped

15 ounces (450 g) baby squid and baby
  octopus
1½ cups (350 g) risotto rice
5 tablespoons (75 ml) white wine
Salt and black pepper

1	Bring the squid ink and fish stock to a boil in a pan. Allow it to reduce then keep it simmering over low heat.	2	Melt the butter in a medium heavy-based non-stick saucepan and gently cook the shallots and garlic until soft.
3	Chop the seafood, then add into the pan and gently cook for 3–4 minutes until tender.	4	Add the rice and coat in the butter. Pour in the wine and simmer until most of it has been absorbed by the rice. ➤

	Add the squid ink stock, a ladleful at a time, until all the stock has been absorbed by the rice. Keep on low heat stirring continuously for 20 minutes until the rice is creamy but al dente.	**TIP** ❋
5		You can get the squid ink from the fishmonger.

6	Season to taste with salt and pepper, add the remaining butter and sprinkle with shavings of Parmesan cheese to serve.	**NOTE** ❋ Serve with a mixed salad, if you like.

BAKED CRAB WITH HERB CRUST

❧ SERVES 4 • PREPARATION : 10 MINUTES • COOKING : 1–2 MINUTES ❧

1¾ ounces (50 g) brown crabmeat
3½ ounces (100 g) white crabmeat
2 tablespoons (25 g) butter, melted
Juice of ½ lemon
1 teaspoon wholegrain mustard
Pinch of paprika

Salt and black pepper
4 small crab shells

HERB CRUST :
¼ cup (30 g) white breadcrumbs
1 tablespoon (15 ml) butter, melted

¼ cup (25 g) Parmesan cheese, grated
1 tablespoon (15 g) chopped parsley
1 tablespoon (15 g) chopped chives

IN ADVANCE :
Preheat the grill to medium.

1 2
3 4

1	Put all the crabmeat into a large bowl, add the melted butter, lemon juice, mustard, paprika, seasoning and mix together.	2	Spoon the crab mix into the crab shells and put onto a baking tray.	
3	For the herb crust, mix the breadcrumbs, butter and cheese together thoroughly in a bowl.	4	Add the parsley and chives to the bread-crumbs, and season.	➤

5 Spread the breadcrumb mixture over the crabmeat and cook under the hot grill for about 1–2 minutes, or until golden.

VARIATION
❁

Use brown shrimp instead of brown crabmeat.

6	Serve the crabs immediately with steamed asparagus.	❋ Serve with a mixed salad instead of asparagus, if you like.

BROWN SHRIMP FRITTATA

✦ SERVES 2 • PREPARATION : 5 MINUTES • COOKING : 6–8 MINUTES ✦

1 tablespoon (15 ml) olive oil
2 tablespoons (25 g) butter
3½ ounces (100 g) cooked baby potatoes,
   sliced
1 garlic clove, finely chopped

5 ounces (150 g) peeled brown shrimp
5 eggs
⅓ cup (30 g) Parmesan cheese, grated
1 tablespoon chopped chives
Salt and black pepper

IN ADVANCE :
Preheat the oven to 400°F (200°C).

1 2
3 4

1	Heat the oil and butter in a large ovenproof frying pan, add in the potatoes, garlic and shrimp and cook for 30 seconds.	2	In a large bowl, beat the eggs with the grated Parmesan, chopped chives and a good pinch of salt and pepper.
3	Pour the eggs into the pan on top of the shrimps and once the mixture has started to set at the bottom transfer to the hot oven.	4	Remove from the oven after 6–8 minutes once it is golden on top. Serve with summer vegetables.

LOBSTER WITH CAYENNE

SERVES 2 • PREPARATION : 5 MINUTES • COOKING : 8 MINUTES

2 pounds (1 kg) fresh live lobster
2 tablespoons (30 g) butter, melted
Sea salt and black pepper
1 teaspoon cayenne pepper
1 lemon

IN ADVANCE :

Putting the lobster in a freezer for 2 hours is recommended as the most humane way to kill a lobster.

Preheat the grill to high.

TIP :

Cook the lobster for 4 minutes on each side. This is also a great way to cook lobster in the summer on the barbecue.

1	Lay the lobster belly-side down on a board and cut it lengthwise in half.	2	Remove the stomach sac, a pouch in the head section, from each half.	3	Remove the intestinal vein from the tail section.
4	Remove any bands from the claws and bash to help the claws cook faster.	5	Brush with butter; season; sprinkle with cayenne; grill for 8 minutes with lemon.	6	Serve the lobster with any remaining butter, the lemon halves and salad.

CRAB IN BLACK BEAN SAUCE

❧ SERVES 2–4 • PREPARATION : 5–10 MINUTES • COOKING : 8–10 MINUTES ❧

8–10 blue swimmer crabs cut in half and
   cleaned by the fishmonger
1 large knob of ginger
8 green onions
3 shallots

1 lemon
1 tablespoon (15 g) black beans, chopped
1 tablespoon (15 ml) sesame oil

IN ADVANCE :

Put a metal petal steamer in a shallow pan
   with a tight-fitting lid and fill the pan
   halfway up with water.

1 2
3 4

1	Break off the claws from the crabs.	2	Finely slice the ginger, green onions and shallots.
3	In a small bowl, mix the juice of the lemon with the black beans and sesame oil.	4	Put the crabs in a steamer and arrange the green onions and shallots around the sides. ➤

5

Add the black bean sauce, then cover and steam the crabs for about 8–10 minutes.

TIP
❋

This recipe also works well with medium-sized sea bass fillets.

6 Serve the crabs with some of the juices poured over them and accompanied with lime wedges and sliced red chili.

NOTE
❋
For extra flavor. steam with beer instead of water.

PAN-FRIED SHRIMP

❧ SERVES 2–3 • PREPARATION : 5 MINUTES • COOKING : 2–3 MINUTES ❧

½ teaspoon superfine sugar
1 tablespoon (15 ml) dark soy sauce
1 teaspoon cornflour
2 tablespoons (30 ml) Chinese rice wine
1 tablespoon (15 ml) vegetable oil, for frying
1 red chili, thinly sliced

¾ cup (50 g) lemongrass, crushed and finely
   chopped
½ cup (100 g) green onions, cut into pieces
12 large raw shrimp, butterflied (see
   butterflying shrimp, 59) with tail on
¼ cup (50 ml) chicken stock

IN ADVANCE :
Heat a wok over medium heat.

1 2
3 4

1	Mix the sugar, soy sauce, cornflour and Chinese rice wine together in a bowl.	2	Add a little oil to the hot wok, then add the chili, lemongrass and green onions and fry for a few seconds.
3	Add the shrimp together with the soy sauce mixture. Pour in the stock, then cover and cook for 2–3 minutes.	4	Serve with cooked fragrant Thai rice.

APPENDIXES

BASIC SAUCES

GLOSSARY

FISH FACTS GLOSSARY

RECIPE INDEX

GENERAL INDEX

ACKNOWLEDGMENTS

BASIC SAUCES

TARTAR SAUCE

200ml/7fl oz mayonnaise
Squeeze of lemon juice
3 tablespoons chopped capers
3 tablespoons chopped gherkins
1 small shallot, finely chopped
3 tablespoons chopped parsley
Sea salt and black pepper

1 Mix all of the ingredients together in a small bowl.

2 Serve immediately with fish of your choice. This sauce works well with smoked haddock fish cakes, 55; crisp chilli salt sprats, 32; goujons of sole, 40.

TIP : Store in the refrigerator until needed and keeps for 2 days.

AIOLI

3 free-range egg yolks
150ml/5fl oz extra virgin olive oil
4 garlic cloves, finely chopped
Juice of ½ lemon
Salt and black pepper
1 teaspoon Dijon mustard

1 Blend all the ingredients, except the olive oil, in a food processor.

2 Pour the oil into the blender in a steady stream until it forms a thick sauce.

3 Serve with the fish dish of your choice. The mixture, once blended, should be vibrant and yellow in color. If you'd like your sauce a bit runnier, add a couple of tablespoons of hot water. It works well with herb-crusted cod, 35; Maryland crab cake, 78 and pan-fried trout, 43.

TIP : You can add garlic, lemon and Dijon mustard to a good-quality mayonnaise to create an aioli.

CHILI SAUCE

2 tablespoons Thai fish sauce
5 tablespoons green onions, thinly sliced
3 tablespoons lime juice or lemon juice
6 red Serrano chilies, finely chopped
½ teaspoon finely chopped garlic

1 Combine all the ingredients in a small bowl and mix well.

2 Serve with fish of your choice. It works well with prawns wrapped in noodles, 61; fish tempura, 37; goujons of sole, 40; beer-battered oysters, 71 and crispy soft-shelled crabs, 67.

TIP : Can be kept in the refrigerator for 1 week.

WHITE/BÉCHAMEL SAUCE

750ml/24fl oz/3 cups milk
10 whole black peppercorns
1 bay leaf
50g/1¾oz unsalted butter
75g/2½oz plain flour
2 teaspoons Dijon mustard
Salt and black pepper

1 Put the milk in a saucepan with the peppercorns and bay leaf.

2 Bring to a boil, then turn off the heat and infuse for 10 minutes. Strain.

3 Melt the butter in a saucepan, stir in the flour and cook for 1–2 minutes.

4 Gradually stir in the infused milk, bit by bit, to get a smooth sauce.

5 Simmer gently for 1–2 minutes, add the Dijon mustard and season with salt and pepper.

TIP : This recipe is used in the fish pie, 54, but is delicious served with any pan-fried or steamed white fish.

GLOSSARY

Carpaccio – This is when raw meat or fish is very thinly sliced, especially beef or tuna, and then garnished with a sauce.

Ceviche – Raw fish or seafood that is pickled and "cooked" in the acidic juices of citrus fruit. Ceviches can be flavored with herbs, chillies and other ingredients, and they are commonly served as a starter.

Debearded mussels – Most mussels have what is commonly termed "the beard", also called byssal threads. The beard is comprised of many fibers that emerge from the mussel's shell. To remove the beard, grasp the beard and give a sharp yank out and towards the hinge end of the mussel. This method will not kill the mussel. Discard the byssal threads.

En papillote – A method of cooking in which the fish is put into a folded pouch or parcel and then baked. The translation from French is "in parchment". The parcel can be made with parchment or foil.

Flat fish – A classification of fish based on skeletal type, characterized by its flat body and both eyes on one side of its head. Types of this fish include: plaice, lemon sole, flounder, halibut, turbot and brill.

Gravlax – Originally a Nordic dish, it is a way of curing raw salmon in salt, sugar and dill. It is then thinly sliced and generally served as a starter.

Gumbo – This is a stew or soup originally from Louisiana. It consists primarily of a strong stock, meat or shellfish and vegetables.

Pin boning – To pin bone fish, gently run your fingers over the surface of the fillet and remove any small bones you find with a pair of tweezers. You can pin bone either before or after cooking.

Round fish – A classification of fish based on skeletal type, characterized by eyes on opposite sides of its head, a backbone along its upper body with a fillet located on both sides. Types of this fish include: trout, bass, cod, pike, snapper and salmon.

Scaling – This is the removal of the scales from the fish using a fish scaler. This will always be done by the fishmonger prior to purchase. Sometimes store-bought fish may still have scales attached, so remove gently with a fish scaler. However, if you are removing the skin this won't be a problem.

Tempura – A Japanese specialty prepared by deep-frying fish that has been dipped in tempura batter. The batter is light, thin and crispy, due to being made with soda water, or light beer.

Test of fresh fish – When buying fish, whether from a supermarket or from a fishmonger, look out for a couple of things. Firstly, the eyes on a whole fish should look glossy, if they look dark it's an indication of an old fish. Secondly, fish should not have a pungent smell. If the fish does have a strong smell it usually indicates the fish is not very fresh.

Unopened mussels – If some of your mussels have not opened after cooking, then it is possible that either they were not cooked long enough, or they are bad and should be discarded.

Undyed fish – Traditionally, haddock is brined, soaked in salted water and smoked over a wood fire, giving the fish a pale yellow color. Nowadays, much of the dyed haddock is smoked using machinery instead of real smoke. It's then dyed with coloring to resemble the traditional version. Undyed smoked haddock is produced in the same way but there's no coloring added so the fish taste remains the same whether dyed or undyed.

FISH FACTS GLOSSARY

When shopping, a good supply of fish is usually readily available. Depending on the time of year and on fishing stocks, prices may vary with some of the less available fish having a higher price. However, recently it has been noted that because some fish types in the past were more sought after than other fish, supplies of these fish are depleting rapidly, with fishermen forced to go to greater lengths to obtain them. Such fish have become endangered and the fish listed below are most vulnerable to over-fishing or are fished using methods that cause damage to the environment.

SUSTAINABLE FISH & SEAFOOD – WHAT TO EAT & WHAT TO AVOID

SPECIES	EAT	AVOID
BREAM	✓ Black bream: gill net, line caught	
CLAMS	✓ Manila & Carpet shell	
COCKLES	✓ Hand gathered	
COD	✓ Atlantic: NE Arctic, Eastern Baltic, Iceland ✓ Pacific: Alaska, Aleutian Islands	✕ Atlantic: All other sources except occasionally Western Baltic, Faroe Plateau ✕ Pacific: All other sources
COLEY	✓ North Sea, W Scotland & Rockall, NE Arctic	
CRAB	✓ Spider: pot-caught	
DAB	✓ Otter trawled, seine net caught	
EEL		✕ European & Conger
FLOUNDER	✓ Otter trawled, gill net caught	
GURNARD	✓ Grey & Red	
HADDOCK	✓ NE Arctic, North Sea, Rockall	✕ W Scotland & Faroes
HAKE	✓ Only eat occasionally	
HALIBUT	✓ Atlantic: Farmed (onshorwe production)	✕ Atlantic: wild caught only
HERRING	✓	✕ W Ireland & Western Baltic
LING	✓ Only eat occasionally if longline or gill net caught	✕ All other sources
LOBSTER	✓ Only eat occasionally	✕ American: Southern New England
MACKEREL	✓ All sources	
MUSSELS	✓ Farmed or hand gathered	
OYSTERS	✓ Farmed	

SPECIES	EAT	AVOID
PLAICE	✓ Only eat other sources occasionally	✕ Baltic & Celtic Seas, English Channel, SW & W Ireland
POLLACK	✓ All sources except eat trawled occasionally	
PRAWNS	✓ Tiger & King (organically farmed)	✕ Tiger & King: wild caught & non-certified farmed
RAY		✕ All Blonde, Sandy, Shagreen & Undulate rays
RED MULLET	✓ All sources	
SALMON	✓ Pacific & Atlantic (organically farmed)	✕ Atlantic: wild caught
SARDINE/PILCHARD	✓ All sources except eat Med & Bay of Biscay occasionally	
SCALLOP	✓ King: diver-caught Queen: otter-trawled	
SCAMPI/DUBLIN BAY PRAWNS	✓ All sources only eat occasionally	
SEA BASS	✓ All other sources except eat farmed occasionally	✕ Pelagic trawled
SHARK	✓ Eat lesser-spotted dogfish occasionally	✕ Shark, spurdog
SKATE		✕ All skate
SOLE	✓ Lemon: All sources except eat trawled occasionally	✕ Dover: SW & W Ireland, Irish Sea, W English Channel
SQUID	✓ Jig caught, can eat trawled occasionally	
SWORDFISH	✓ Harpoon (NE Pacific)	✕ Indian Ocean, Med, S Atlantic, NW Pacific
TILAPIA	✓ Farmed (organic or closed production)	
TROUT	✓ Rainbow: Organic farmed or freshwater ponds	✕ Brown or Sea: wild caught from Baltic
TUNA	✓ Albacore: Pole & line caught or troll caught from S Pacific ✓ Skipjack: Pole & line caught, Pacific, W Atlantic or Maldives	✕ Albacore: N Atlantic, Med ✕ Bigeye: Indian Ocean, Atlantic & Central W Pacific ✕ Bluefin: All sources
TURBOT	✓ Farmed (onshore production)	✕ Beam trawl caught

GENERAL INDEX

INDEX OF RECIPES

DEDICATION

To Mum, Dad and all the family for your continual encouragement

ACKNOWLEDGMENTS

My thanks to my amazing family for their love, support and help over the years; to Ben, Kirsty, Daniel, Rosea, Samuel, Rachel, Will, Nathan, Naomi, Hanna, Jacob and to Auntie Anne and Zak and family.

Big thanks to Rebecca Fawcett for her constant help and support, couldn't have done it without ya! To Kate McCullough and Yasmin Othman thanks for your help. Thanks goes to Deirdre for all of the beautiful photographs and hours of processing. With a big thank you to Catie Ziller and with special thanks for the editorial and design work of Kathy Steer and Alice Chadwick.

I would like to thank all the people I met and enjoyed the company of on my trip to Australia, especially the times shared with my Uncle Peter and Auntie Jean, Bruce, Sheila and Emma and Jay and their families. It was a truly inspiring trip with so many amazing flavours and wonderful seafood.

And thanks to all those who have helped me along the way; Anna P, Anna J, Anna H, Anthony, Christina, Colette, Emily, Fions, Gary, Ginny, Georgie, Jeff, Karen, Kate, Kevin, Lisa, Laura, Paul R, Ruth, Sarah, Sioban, Sharri-Sue and Sole.

Thanks for all the wonderful fresh fish from Daily Fish supplies.

Thanks to the Marine Conservation Society (MCS) for giving us permission to use the chart on the fish facts glossary page. See www.mcsuk.org and www.goodfishguide.co.uk for more details.